Lisa Shipley

Lisa Ship... (signature)

Movie Inspired Meals
Cookbook & Trivia Game

When a movie buff and a Chef fall in love...

Written by: Lisa Shipley and James Shipley

Edited by: Lisa Shipley

Shipley Publishing

Shipley Publishing

www.shipleypublishing.com

Editing by Lisa Shipley

Cover Design by Lisa Shipley and James Shipley

Content by Lisa Shipley and James Shipley

ISBN-13: 978-0615939223 (Shipley Publishing)

ISBN-10: 0615939228

Contents

Preface

Their Idea: When a movie buff and a Chef fall in love...

Ideas are powerful if you are bold enough to share those, so they discussed their thoughts and passions until the architecture was in place to house their visions...

Whenever she talked with him about food items mentioned in movies that she adores, he was inspired to create entire meals based upon those ideas. He wrote the recipes and cooked the meals, and then they dined with incredible movie-inspired meals while watching those movies.

One evening, over dessert, they discussed how much fun they had combining movies with meals and how other people would enjoy this new twist on dinner and a movie too. This was the birth of the idea for this book.

Ideas are powerful if given focus and direction, so they started to plan and to work...

As a Chef and author, he is amazing at offering recipes that taste awesome and can be created at home by beginners. As a movie buff and editor, she gives him the inspiration, tests meals, does the dishes, translates his "Chef speak" for the recipes, and edits his books.

Ideas are powerful if given support, so they created a project on kickstarter.com to obtain the financial support needed to create this cookbook...

The project received 37 Kickstarter backers, who made the project a possibility, and we thank you. You, who believed in our vision and in our potential to fulfill that vision with this book.

Ideas are powerful if given a voice to communicate...

Each movie inspired item was crafted into a meal of three courses (appetizer, entree, dessert) which complement each other. Each meal was designed to serve four people so that you can share the fun with family and friends.

The MIM Trivia Game was crafted with hints of different difficulty levels, to see if you can guess the movie that inspired a recipe from each meal. The mess was formed into a book draft, then Lisa did the editing (and the dinner dishes!) until everything was as it should be.

The Result of the Idea...

We are delighted to offer this unique book to you. We strive to find work that always inspires us and continues our journey to learn, try, fail, postpone, succeed, and love together. We hope you not only enjoy this book enough to share it with your family and friends, but we also hope to become people who you want to follow for sharing in our future projects. You can follow us on Facebook and on our websites: www.shipleypublishing.com and www.twobearschocolates.com

Acknowledgments

I would like to thank James Shipley. James, you are my inspiration, my best friend, my husband, my home, my joy, and my hero, and I love you! Come what may, let's go find another adventure! I trust you.

I would like to thank my oldest sister, Lorri, my middle sister, Linda, and my nieces, Kelli, Nikki, Kristi, and Jessi for sharing in the excitement of this idea, in the delight of reading, and in the wonder that is in movies.

Lisa Shipley

I would like to thank Lisa Shipley, my editor and co-author, wife, and best friend. I love you.

Thank you to my grandmother, Genevieve Raschick, an amazing cook, baker, and role model. May you rest in peace.

James Shipley

Together, we would like to thank all the people who believed in this project before we even started cooking and writing. You are our "Kickstarter" backers, through www.kickstarter.com.

Finally, thank you to Eowynn, our 10 year old puppy, who is a Newfoundland mixed breed. Eowynn is who sits beside us for every moment of writing and cooking, who takes us outside for walks, and who is always game for a snuggle break.

James and Lisa

Acknowledged for Awesomeness*

*the following awesome people were the backers on our Kickstarter project who chose the highest levels of sponsorship, and we thank you for your outstanding awesomeness in supporting this book and us!

Lorri Holser

Shelly

Pam S. Heintz

Introduction

Welcome to the inspired meals side of

Movie Inspired Meals Cookbook!

Food inspiration is universal. The goal of this book is to give you simple success with inspired meals, many with international roots, and to do so with the same patience and simplicity of our Beginners Guide series of cookbooks. We want your global food knowledge to grow and to guide you to better understand pairings of dishes into a three course meal whether using complimentary or contradictory flavors to enhance the entire meal experience.

Before you begin making inspired meal recipes, please read over the informational sections as there are important details found there to guide you to meal awesomeness. For example, we discuss ingredients in a section to help you read and measure for each recipe.

Ingredient information will also make the aisles at the store less confusing for purchases. For those of you who have limited access to unique and international food items, we have recommendations on purchasing those items online from reputable sources.

Some inspired meals include bread as a side dish or an appetizer, but we enjoy bread with most of our meals and thus recommend our Bread: A Beginners Guide cookbook if you want more bread recipes to accompany all of your inspired cooking.

We do not use weight measurements for the ingredients in this book. Instead, we use volume measurements and for a very specific reason: we want this book to be accessible, to be comfy. Professional recipes use only weight, but understand that even weight measurement recipes depend on conditions like humidity, ingredient quality, elevation, temperature, and the individual cook or baker. Using weight does not guarantee accuracy.

Using careful **volume** measurements that we explain in the ingredients section will make you accurate enough for the recipes we have designed.

The recipes in this book have been streamlined to be as quick as possible. We do this to make cooking and baking less intimidating and to make it fit within any busy lifestyle. After you have taken the time to cook and bake your way through many of these recipes and feel confident about your kitchen skills, we encourage you to try some of the more involved preparations in professional books and compare results.

Additionally, we hope that this book will introduce you or reminded you of some amazing food and incredible films: old and new, obscure and popular, US and international. Be inspired, be groovy.

James and Lisa

How the MIM Trivia Game is Played

Welcome to the inspirational movies game side

(aka MIM Trivia Game) of

Movie Inspired Meals Cookbook!

Each of our 3-course (appetizer, entree, dessert) meals incorporates 1 course or course's main dish that was inspired by a movie. The **MIM Trivia Game** is to review the 3 courses, then use your knowledge of movies to discover the inspired course and the inspirational film.

Keep in mind:

➢ There are 3 courses to every meal, so any 1 of those courses could be the inspired course.

➢ Only 1 course is inspired, and the other 2 courses are just what we believe are wonderful accompaniments to the inspired course.

➤ An entree course's main dish may have a side dish that is paired with it, but a side dish alone will not be the inspired dish within the entree course. For example, if the entree course is spaghetti with meatballs and a side of steamed vegetables and garlic bread - the vegetables cannot be the inspired dish by itself, but the spaghetti with meatballs main dish might be. You would consider the entree course's main dish (spaghetti and meatballs), the appetizer, and the dessert as options for the one that was inspired.

➤ The course is an inspired course, which is not always the exact one used in the movie.

➤ The inspirational item may not even be seen in the movie but rather a key ingredient or dish mentioned in a moment that makes it memorable.

➤ If we used our artistic license to create a dish that is inspired from a key ingredient mentioned in the movie, then we've used that item as a major focus and used it in the name of the dish.

For example, if a key ingredient mentioned or used in a memorable part in the movie is mango, then we could make the mango chicken over plantains dish mentioned earlier.

No recipe is copied directly from any movie, rather we used the movies as inspiration to create our own recipes, the same as when any other artist is inspired by something seen or heard but then makes a personally interpreted creation.

The MIM Trivia Game has multiple levels of clues.

The first round has no trivia clues but is just guessed after learning the names of the 3 courses.

The second round has the first level of trivia and is the hardest, as we only provide you with a clue about an un-named dish being in a particular scene or associated with a particular portion of the movie.

The trivia hint here will be enough for a movie buff-foodie to guess the inspirational movie, but for those will who only focus on one or the other, the next level will be more accessible to you.

The third round has the second level of clues, which will mostly relate to the inspirational movie in general other with food-related references, as you may be a movie buff and have knowledge of the movie but were never drawn to remember our chosen inspirational food. These will not be easy clues, as we want only true movie and foodie buffs to discover the inspirational movie at this level.

For the fourth round, we will offer a third level of easier trivia and h ints AND tell you which dish is the inspired dish, as this game should be fun for those who are entry-level movie buffs and foodies, not just those of us who seek out movies with great food references. Most people who have seen the inspirational movie will have a strong chance at knowing the answer.

Our idea on how to play the MIM Trivia Game when you are cooking a Movie Inspired Meal:

Round One, tell all of the players what the 3 courses are and have players write down 1 movie choice they think is the inspiration. We suggest scrap paper or entry on a smartphone "notepad" to be "green".

Round Two, tell all of the players the first level of clues and have players write down one movie choice - it may be the same or a different choice than before.

Round Three, tell all of the players the second level of clues and have players write down one movie choice - again it may be the same or a different choice than before.

Round Four, tell all of the players the third level of clues and have players write down one movie choice - again it may be the same or a different choice than before.

Then, the answers section for the inspirational movie and score your players accordingly to the round that the correct answer was given. Add all of each player's round points for their MIM Trivia Game total score. Total potential for all four rounds: 200

Round One Correct: 100

Round Two Correct: 60

Round Three Correct: 30

Round Four Correct: 10

Love the MIM Trivia Game?

Then, play, watch, and cook through the whole Movie Inspired Meals Cookbook and declare among yourselves a MIM Master! Just until December 31, 2014, contact us on the www.shipleypublishing.com site regarding who your MIM Master is, and we'll put that person's name on the website, along with the score that person achieved for the total book. Please be sure to get that person's permission before offering us a name for posting on www.shipleypublishing.com. Also, "names" will be subject to approval by James Shipley and Lisa Shipley before being posted on www.shipleypublishing.com.

There are some "popular" foodie/movie buff movies that we decided to exclude from this book. Why?

If we did not personally find redeeming value for inspiration in a movie, then we were not going to use it. We used movies that truly inspired the creation of a dish that we could use in a designing a meal. No inspiration = not in here. We hope that you enjoy the recipes and the MIM Trivia game as much as we have enjoyed creating these!

Good luck with the MIM Trivia Game!

Several wonderful Kickstarter sponsors invested something extra, their time, in verifying that the MIM Trivia Game is easy to understand and fun for people of all playing levels to enjoy. Our gratitude goes to:

Anonymous

Bernie De Santis III

Elizabeth

Erin T.

Terry Elvers

Ingredients

...and How to Measure / Prepare Each

Measuring Tip: Any time you are measuring and have a heaping amount to level off, place a plate, bowl, or similar item under your measuring work area to catch the excess that you level off. The excess can be returned to the original container to eliminate a waste of ingredients.

Baking Powder and Baking Soda:

Make sure these are no more than six months old! If these are not fresh, these will not work as effectively.

Measure these by scooping a heaping amount out of the container with the appropriate size measuring spoon, then use a flat edge (like a table knife) to remove the excess, leaving a smooth, leveled amount for an exact measurement.

Cooks outside the US, please reference the conversion chart.

Flour:

There are many types of flour available in grocery markets. I want to clarify the difference between three of the major flours to avoid confusion when you purchase your flours.

First, there is pastry flour, which is also called cake flour. We will not be using this flour for recipes in this book, and it is not an acceptable substitute.

Second, there is AP or All-Purpose flour. It is between a very low-gluten pastry flour and high-gluten bread flour. For baking, AP can be used in pastry recipes and may be used in some making bread recipes, but only if specified as an acceptable substitute. Finally, if you are not baking and the recipe specifies AP flour, then do not use a substitute, as the ratios in the recipe have been determined based upon the nature and known reactions of AP flour. If the type of flour is not specified in a recipe, then use AP flour.

Third, bread flour can also be called high-gluten flour, because its defining feature is its high gluten content, which provides the structure for making great bread.

Flours are broken down further by their source, such as whole wheat, rye, sunflower, rice, etc. When purchasing flour for a recipe, check for both the type of flour and the source of the flour to get the correct one.

Measure flour by putting the appropriate sized measuring cup on a flat surface, then pour the flour from its original container into the cup until it is heaping. Then, use a flat edge (like a table knife) to remove the excess, leaving a smooth and leveled amount for an exact measurement. Do NOT scoop the flour from the container, as this can compact/pack the floor and end up with you measuring too much. Do NOT shake the measuring cup to level off the flour, as this may also result in settling/packing of flour and end up with you measuring too much.

Cooks outside the US, please reference the conversion chart.

Eggs:

Check eggs for stamped expiration date first. Then, check the freshness by cracking one egg onto a plate: if the two parts stay close together, then the egg is fresh. The farther the two parts spread apart, the older the egg is. Fresh eggs are vital for the recipe process to be successful.

Cracking an egg: Hold the egg gently in one hand, exposing a "side" of the egg, then use a flat surface, **not an edge**, to tap lightly once, on one side of the egg. Next, hold the egg over a bowl, place the tips of your thumbs into the indent/break in the shell, and in a combined motion, pull the shell apart and upwards, allowing the entire egg contents to drop into the bowl. Toss the shell into the trash bin. Repeat for remaining needed eggs. Wash hands before moving on, as the shell is where salmonella and other "baddies" live.

Always crack eggs into a separate bowl before adding into a bowl with other ingredients. In case you have a "bad" one, you just have to replace your eggs and not all the ingredients in use up to that point.

Separating an egg: After an egg is cracked and in a bowl, cup one hand with fingers tightly closed and gently transfer the egg into that hand. Place the bowl under the cupped hand, and slightly open your fingers to allow just the "white" part to slip through and into the bowl, all the while, keeping the "yellow" yolk in your hand. Transfer the yolk into another bowl and set aside. Save the "white" part in a covered bowl in the refrigerator for other uses like breakfast eggs or in making a meringue topping.

Use "large" eggs as standard sized in US stores.

Cooks outside the US, please reference the conversion chart.

Butter:

Use unsalted butter. We can always add the exact amount of salt needed for each recipe if we know that we are starting out with a standard amount of zero salt in the butter. Check the expiration date as fresh butter is important.

Measure butter either with the "marked" 1/4 pound sticks or firmly pack butter into the appropriate size measuring cup.

Cooks outside the US, please reference the conversion chart.

Yeast:

Instant dried yeast is the one we use for all recipes, and this is the little packets common in US grocery stores. Check the expiration date for freshness.

Yeast options are given in the conversion chart section in case you want to use a different style and have it work the same as the instant dried in all of my recipes.

Measure by scooping a heaping amount out of the container with the appropriate size measuring spoon, then use a flat edge (like a table knife) to remove the excess, leaving a smooth, leveled amount for an exact measurement.

Cooks outside the US, please reference the conversion chart.

Milk:

Use whole bovine (cow) milk, also known as Vitamin D or full-fat, unless specified, such as heavy cream. Check the expiration date, then smell and visually inspect milk for freshness.

Measure into appropriate size measuring cup, using a flat surface for a level measurement and viewing at eye level.

When a substitute is appropriate, we will use specific information on the type of alternative milk product and the changes to the quantities.

Cooks outside the US, please reference the conversion chart.

Graham Cracker Crumbs:

These can be purchased pre-crushed in most baking aisles, or you can crush these yourself. To crush graham crackers, place crackers into a plastic bag or between folded parchment paper and press down with a dough-pin / rolling-pin or press and grind with a sturdy glass piece such as a measuring cup.

Heavy Cream:

Heavy cream (bovine) can be packaged as "whipping cream".

Measure into appropriate size measuring cup, using a flat surface for a level measurement and viewing at eye level.

Honey:

Honey changes flavor depending upon seasons, regions, and if organic, so use this ingredient to add personal preference flavors to your breads.

Before measuring honey, mist/spritz the spoon or cup with non-stick cooking oil. To measure, pour or scrape into the measuring spoon or cup until a level amount is achieved, viewing at eye level. The oil mist will release the honey into the mix much easier allowing for a more accurate measurement and for easier cleaning of the measuring device afterwards.

Cooks outside the US, please reference the conversion chart.

Sugar:

Use white, granulated sugar unless otherwise specified.

Measure sugar by scooping a heaping amount out of the container with the appropriate size measuring spoon / cup, then use a flat edge (like a table knife) to remove the excess, leaving a smooth, leveled amount for an exact measurement.

Cooks outside the US, please reference the conversion chart.

Salt:

Use non-iodized Kosher or Sea salt.

Measure by scooping a heaping amount out of the container with the appropriate size measuring spoon, then use a flat edge (like a table knife) to remove the excess, leaving a smooth, leveled amount for an exact measurement.

Cooks outside the US, please reference the conversion chart.

Warm Water:

Water should be warmed to between 80 - 100 degrees. To check this, we recommend using a cooking thermometer. Without a thermometer, you can test it with your wrist, BUT you risk burning yourself and not having an accurate result. For bread-specific recipes: For the wrist method, if it the water feels comfortably warm on your wrist then it is not too warm for yeast. If your water is too hot, then it will kill yeast and not make your bread.

Why test with the wrist and not fingers? Fingers are usually less sensitive to temperature, while wrists are more likely to be accurate. We recommend using a thermometer, especially as it can be used later to help you in determining when breads and meats are done, etc.

For a thermometer, make sure that it is very clean and is calibrated before each use. To check its calibration accuracy, place the thermometer in a pot of boiling water. The water should be at a steady boil, and the tip of the baking / candy thermometer should not touch the bottom of the pan. Wait for three minutes, then check the reading and make sure to read the temperature straight on (don't look down or up at the thermometer). It should read 212 F/ 100 C. If there is a difference from this compared to the temperature showing on the thermometer, then you can use the thermometer, as long as you make sure you take this difference into account and adjust the your desired temperature by the number of calibrated degrees over or under.

Measure warm water into appropriate size measuring cup / spoon, until a level measurement is achieved, viewing at eye level.

Cooks outside the US, please reference the conversion chart.

Vanilla Extract:

Use a PURE vanilla extract. Do NOT use artificial vanilla. When making any recipe, the product can only be as amazing as the least awesome ingredient. Vanilla extracts change flavor depending upon the region the beans are from, if it is extracted using organic ingredients, and how long it has aged, so use this ingredient to add personal flavors to your recipes.

If you want to try our custom vanilla extracts, then contact us for what we have available for purchase through our business as www.twobearschocolates.com. We use only vanilla beans, alcohol, and time to produce vanilla extracts.

Measure extract into appropriate size measuring spoon, until a level measurement is achieved, viewing at eye level.

Cooks outside the US, please reference the conversion chart.

Juicing an Orange / Lemon:

Rinse the fruit under cold water and dry it. Roll the whole fruit around on a clean table, using the palm of your hand, with firm pressure, as this allows the juices to begin releasing inside the fruit for easier removal. Transfer fruit to a cutting board, then use a knife to cut the fruit in half "going around the middle" (**not** going through the "navel" or the stem / nub). Set aside. Place a mesh strainer over a bowl. With bare hands, squeeze the fruit half over the strainer, as this allows the pulp and membranes to be kept out of the juice and transfer to the trash bin. Juiced citrus can be kept in the bowl, covered with plastic wrap / film for up to 3 days.

Zesting an Orange / Lemon:

If you do not have a micro-plane or zester tool, then you can use a vegetable / potato peeler or a carrot / cheese grater tool. Rinse the fruit under cold water and dry it with a clean towel. Then, with a tool, remove just the orange / yellow outermost layer of the fruit, being careful to not remove the white layer underneath. The white layer is the pith (rhymes with "with") and is bitter. Go around the fruit in one direction and only move the fruit against the tool in one direction, not back and forth. Remove all of the colored layer. If you used a micro-plane or zester, then you are done. If you used an alternate tool, then transfer peelings / gratings to a cutting board and use a knife to mince. "Finely minced zest" is about the same size as coarse sea salt. Keep the fruit without its peel in a plastic sealable bag for up to 1 week. Use the zest within the same day as it is removed.

Candied Ginger:

Candied ginger is normally sold near dried fruits. There will be many pieces in a plastic container. These mince best if you place one piece at a time on the cutting board. Then, with a sharp knife, slice lengthwise, in super thin strips all the way across. Turn the board 90 degrees, and then cut in super thin pieces until all strips are minced. Freezing candied ginger for a little bit before cutting can reduce the stickiness and keep it firmer for easier cutting.

Measure the minced bits in a measuring spoon of appropriate size, loosely packed.

Fresh Ginger:

Fresh ginger root is best peeled with the edge of spoon rather than a knife or peeler. Hold the ginger in one open hand and with the other hand, hold the spoon and scrape/draw toward to you firmly but gently, just removing the skin. After a section is peeled, cut the peeled chunk off and place on a cutting board.

Cut the ginger in long strips (matchsticks) then hold together and cut the other direction until in small pieces. Do not place in the processor until cut up! Remaining unpeeled ginger should be loosely wrapped in a paper towel and placed in the refrigerator in the vegetable / crisper drawer.

Tofu:

Tofu needs to be pressed to avoid it being mushy and it adding extra water to the dish you are making. To press tofu: Fold 5 paper towels in half. Place the towels on a countertop or cutting board, layer the block of tofu on top of the towels, then fold 5 more paper towels in half and place on top of the tofu. On top of that stack, add a heavy pot, skillet, or grill press with a full can of vegetables on top of that. Leave the tofu tower for 30 minutes. Remove the weight objects and paper towels, then transfer tofu block to a cutting board for your next step in the recipe you are using.

San-G Soya Sauce:

actual soy (soya) sauce without filler and extra sodium, that is wheat-free – great for gluten-free diets!

In General:

I recommend organic products whenever available, and I urge you to purchase from locally owned stores, co-ops, and farmers whenever possible to encourage small business ownership and responsible agriculture.

Conversion Charts

All measurements in this book are US volume.

US common conversions

1 Tablespoon (Tbsp)	=	3 teaspoons (tsp)
1 Ounce (oz)	=	2 Tbsp
1 Cup	=	8 Ounces (ozs)
1 US Pint (pt)	=	2 Cups
1 US Quart (qt)	=	2 Pints (pts)
1 Gallon	=	4 Quarts (qts)

Please note that 1 tsp US = .83 tsp UK

US to Metric conversions

1/4 tsp	=	1.25 mL
1/2 tsp	=	2.5 mL
1 tsp	=	5 mL
1 Tbsp	=	15 mL
1 Ounce	=	30 mL
1/4 Cup	=	60 mL

1/3 Cup	=	78 mL
1/2 Cup	=	118.2 mL
1 Cup	=	236.5 mL
1 Pint (U.S.)	=	473 mL
1 Quart (U.S.)	=	946 mL
1/2 inch	=	1.27 cm
2 inches	=	5.08 cm
3 inches	=	7.62 cm
15 inches	=	38.1 cm

Fahrenheit to Celsius conversions

300 F	=	148.89 C
325 F	=	162.78 C
350 F	=	176.67 C
375 F	=	190.56 C
400 F	=	204.44 C
425 F	=	218.33 C
450 F	=	232.22 C
500 F	=	260.00 C

Yeast conversions

1 packet (2-1/4 tsp.) active dry is the equivalent to:

1 cube fresh

1 packet quick rise

3/4 packet instant

Egg conversions

1 large egg (US) is approximately 2 oz or 57 g which is equivalent to:

1 large egg (CA)

1 medium egg (EU)

1 large egg (AU)

1 standard "6" egg (NZ)

Tools and Tips

This book is going to teach you to work with normal household kitchen items to make great recipes.

Normal = nothing commercial, nothing intimidating, nothing fancy.

Thermometer:

There is one tool that is absolutely required for our recipes: a kitchen / baking thermometer. Either the traditional or digital style is fine. A few degrees difference in internal temperature is the difference between failure and success with bread and other baking plus this is a key tool for ensuring safe meat products. Check the calibration from time to time.

Calibration: place the end of the thermometer in a pot of boiling water. The water should be at a steady boil, and the tip of the thermometer should NOT touch the bottom of the pan. Wait for a minute, and then check the reading. It should show 212 F / 100 C. If your thermometer shows a different number, then you can still use the thermometer, as long as you make sure you take this difference into account and adjust the recipe temperatures by the number of calibrated degrees over or under.

Pans:

If you do not have bread pans, then you can shape breads and simply bake these on a half-sheet pan (aka cookie sheet or jelly roll pan). For your half-sheet pan, what you are looking for is a heavy sheet. You do not want an air-cushion built in or any other fancy features. Non-stick is okay, but not necessary. For baking pans, your choice of ceramic, silicone, metal, or glass is fine.

If we suggest an alternate pan, such as a ceramic liner of a crock-pot / slow-cooker, then ensure that yours is oven safe before use.

Bench Scraper:

Also known as a dough scraper, a bench scraper is useful for clearing off your work surface and for cutting a piece of dough into multiple pieces for rolls or individual cookies.

Pastry Brush:

Purchase an actual pastry brush, not a paint brush. Make sure that it is only used for baking work. Either natural or silicone bristles are fine. Do not use any brush that has touched paint, and do not use a brush that has been used with seafood and fish, no matter how well it has been washed, just do not use it. Please.

Parchment Paper:

Although not necessary, this useful tool will save you cleaning time. Plus, it will help protect the bottoms of your baked goods from browning too fast.

45

Spritzer Bottle:

Keep an oil mister (spritzer) or spray bottle of non-stick cooking vegetable oil on hand at all times. We have a refillable oil mister pump bottle to save money compared to pre-loaded spray bottles and to save both the environment and our health from the propellants used for aerosol sprays.

Olive Oil:

When to use which kind? Basic Olive Oil is used any time you are going to apply heat to it with cooking or baking. Extra Virgin Olive Oil is used any time that it is not going to be heated, such as when mixed with herbs or balsamic vinegar for dipping bread or when in a salad dressing recipe.

Tips:

Sauté: to cook something(s) in a pan, on medium or medium-high heat, constantly moving contents in the pan by either gently moving pan forward and backward then occasionally flipping the contents over, all while holding the pan's handle, or by gently stirring with a spatula / spoon.

Folding: is when you use a spatula to make a top-to-bottom circle in the bowl to gently combine ingredients and keep things, like whipped cream and meringues, from deflating. Hold the spatula at an angle so that the handle is almost touching the rim of the bowl. Starting along the edge of the bowl farthest away from you, smoothly and gently slide the spatula down the side of the bowl, across the bottom of the bowl, and up the other side of the bowl, then continue along the top of the mixture, until it is folded over on to itself and the spatula is back where you started from.

Adjustments: in your baking and cooking is normal, depending upon your altitude as well the temperature and humidity, which changes throughout the year. Note changes with your recipes as well as the conditions/seasons that inspired these.

Baking and cooking times: are approximations, not laws. The slightest changes in recipes and individual oven calibrations will change times each time you make a recipe. If your dish looks "done" fifteen minutes early, then check the internal temperature with your thermometer. Temperature "done" is more critical for awesomeness than time "done".

Oops, I forgot that I needed ____:
It is best if you set up your ingredients as if you are doing a cooking show on television - measure out everything before you start. This way you ensure you have enough of everything, that eggs are good, etc.

Clean out your pantry:
Remove all the outdated food. All that stuff you have been meaning to get to for the last 5 years? Bin it.

Inventory what you have:

Avoid canned vegetables, (except for tomatoes) and most processed foods. The price for convenience in these kinds of goods is simply too high.

A note from Chef James about Chocolate for recipes:

I am Chef and Chocolatier, so when I discussed chocolate choices in my Chocolate Truffles: A Beginners Guide, I mentioned these points and find these worth repeating.

What counts as chocolate? This question is at the center of a rift between European and American manufacturers. The crux of the argument is cocoa butter. American manufacturers in general have moved to replacing the cocoa butter in chocolate with vegetable oil to increase profits. European producers have strict rules regarding this process.

Much of what Americans consider chocolate may not be called chocolate in Europe. Cocoa butter is essential to great chocolate. When selecting chocolate to work with, you want to look for high cocoa content and no vegetable oil. Much of what is understand to be chocolate is, in fact, merely chocolate flavored. Which chocolate to use? It is important to find a chocolate that tastes great. This is the fun part. Use this as an opportunity to have a great time doing a **chocolate tasting party** with your friends. You can buy bars of chocolate or little tasting squares from chocolates around the world. Try white chocolates, milk chocolates and dark chocolates from across the globe to find out what you like. Keep a sheet of paper handy to make notes about the tasting process. I call these tasting sheets. Start with white, move to milk, and finish with dark. As you taste, have everyone write down what they think. There is no right or wrong, it is all about finding out what you really like.

Some questions to get you started on tasting...
How is the color? The "snap" of the chocolate as you bite into it? Are there floral hints in the smell? What does the smell remind you of? Let the chocolate melt on your tongue and move it around. How does it feel? Is it creamy? Does it linger in the mouth or fade quickly?

What flavors or "notes" do you taste in the chocolate? (does it have notes of fruit or a raisin finish?)

Drink water between each tasting and keep some coffee grounds handy to smell between each tasting to cleanse your palate. Most importantly, have fun. A chocolate tasting is about experiencing new flavors in chocolate. You can't be wrong, plus you are eating chocolate!

Where do you find a great world selection of chocolates? I have several options for you. First is to take a look around. There are tons of websites offering great selections from around the world. Second is to send me an email, and I can put together a tasting box for you. You can reach us at www.twobearschocolates.com Third is to go to a site which I frequently use when I'm itchy for chocolates: www.worldwidechocolate.com. They have loads of sampler packs of chocolates to choose from. You can get individual bars too! I don't get a dime for the shout out. I just appreciate their customer service and breadth of quality chocolates.

Lisa Shipley and James Shipley

Kneading Bread

Lightly shake 1-2 Tbsp flour (same flour as used in the recipe) onto clean countertop in approximately a 12" square area to cover lightly the kneading work surface (called dusting with flour).

Scrape dough out of bowl with spatula into middle of floured area.

Step 1:
Hold your arms outstretched, hands palm up, fingers together, and fingertips touching, and then using the "littlest finger" edge of the hand, scoop under edge of dough farthest away from you, getting a few inches underneath.

Step 2:
Gently and with a smooth motion fold that edge toward you and on top of itself until the edges are close to meeting, then release the edge.

Step 3:

Turn both wrists so that your fingers point away from you, then place the palms of your hands on top of the dough with your wrists at the edge closest to you.

Step 4:

In a combined movement, push dough using only the palms in a forward and slightly downward motion until your arms reach full extension.

Step 5:

Move hands to sides of the dough, rotate hands palm up, with fingers still together, and using fingertips, gently lift edges just enough to rotate the entire dough piece a "1/4 turn" clockwise, noting that you do not have to pick up the entire piece off of the surface.

Step 6: Repeat Step 1 - Step 5 for the recipe's listed time to reach desired consistency.

Helpful Kneading Hints:

Hint 1:

If dough is sticking to your hands/fingers at any point in the kneading process, then first flip the dough over a few times in the flour on the work surface until the sticky parts are covered. Second, if you need more flour than that, then having an extra cup of flour (same as used in the recipe) nearby will allow you to add a little flour at a time to dust overtop the dough until the sticky parts are covered.

Hint 2:

If you get sticky dough on your hands, then remove it by adding a little flour to your hands and rubbing it around in the same motions as washing your hands.

Hint 3:

As you push forward and down, this process should not tear the skin of the dough. The "skin" will get stronger as your kneading process repeats, but continue to be gentle throughout the repeating steps.

Hint 4:

There are two main errors possible with kneading: too much and too little. Of the two, the error of too little is better. Most recipes use bread flour, so dough will develop gluten strands quickly. A few minutes of kneading will produce structural strands to support most breads. Over-kneading can result in too-tough bread.

Hint 5:

We recommend that you make notes about the results and the time spent kneading each recipe so that you can fine tune your recipes to meet your style. Remember, no two people knead bread the same way or at the same pace. You will become quicker as you gain confidence, but correct technique is more important than speed.

Hint 6:

When kneading, be gentle. The dough did not steal your car, so do not make it suffer. Also, you should not be suffering from a few minutes of kneading. Remember that we are just helping it develop gluten, and that this can be a relaxing process with my specific, simplified steps and maybe some groovy background music.

Frequently Used Side Item Recipes

Baguette Bread

Ingredients:

4 & 1/2 cups bread flour

1 & 1/4 tsp active dry yeast

2 cups water, chilled

1 & 3/4 tsp salt

1 Tbsp cornmeal

1/2 cup boiling water

Directions:

Step 1:

In a bowl, add flour, yeast, and chilled water, then stir, until mixed well.

Step 2:

Add salt, then stir, until well mixed.

Step 3:

Cover with plastic wrap / film and transfer to refrigerator for a minimum of 8 hours. Dough can be kept waiting for up to 3 days.

Step 4:
Transfer bowl from refrigerator to countertop and set aside for 2 hours at room temperature.

Step 5:
Lightly dust a half-sheet pan with cornmeal. Set aside.

Step 6:
Knead 2 - 3 minutes. Do not use a mixer. Do not clean the flour from the countertop after kneading. If the flour was used up during kneading, then reapply flour dusting to the countertop.

Step 7:
Cut dough in half.

Step 8:
Cut each half into half again, for a total of 4 pieces of dough.

Step 9:
Take 1 piece of dough and roll into a 16" long, log-shaped dough of even thickness. You may roll this out with your bare hands on the floured countertop, or you may raise your hands above the countertop, with the piece hanging down and roll dough between your hands, flipping the dough and moving your hands to different holding places to roll into a uniform thickness. You may gently stretch the dough as you are rolling it, in order to achieve the desired length of 16" long.

Step 10:
As you finish rolling 1 piece, place it on the half-sheet pan so that all 4 will fit lengthwise, with uniform spacing between each one.

Step 11:
Repeat Steps 9 & 10, until 4 dough pieces are on the baking pan.

Step 12:
Loosely cover the pan with plastic wrap / film. Allow baguette dough pieces to rise, at room temperature, for 1 - 2 hours, until doubled in volume.

Step 13:
Place an oven rack on the lowest position. On that rack, place a cast-iron skillet or similar oven-safe item capable of retaining large amounts of heat for a long period of time.

Step 14:
Place another oven rack to the middle position with nothing on it.

Step 15:
Preheat oven to 500 degrees.

Step 16:
Place the baking pan into the preheated oven, on the middle rack. Have your 1/2 cup of boiling water ready to use.

Attention! Keep in mind that you will need to do the next move quickly but safely, so protect yourself from a possible steam burn by holding your face and body as far away from the oven door area as possible, wearing oven mitts and a long-sleeved shirt. Also, please have anyone, people watching you or in your vicinity, maintain a safe distance from the oven, especially children.

Step 17:
Holding the oven door handle with one hand and the 1/2 cup of boiling water in the other, quickly and carefully pour the water into the cast-iron skillet on the bottom rack, then quickly close the oven door.

Step 18:
Lower the temperature to 475 degrees.

Step 19:
Bake for 12 - 20 minutes, until golden-brown colored on top and register 205 degrees on your thermometer.

Step 20:
Remove the pan from the oven and place on a heat-safe surface, such as your stovetop.

Step 21:

With a spatula, transfer to a wire rack, to cool for 5 minutes.

Fresh Storage:

Once cooled to room temperature, cover the baguettes with plastic wrap / film or place in a plastic sealable bag and store in the refrigerator. May reheat in the oven on a half-sheet pan uncovered. Use within 1 week.

Frozen Storage:

Once cooled to room temperature, cover the baguettes with plastic wrap / film or place in a plastic sealable bag, move to refrigerator until completely cooled, then move to freezer. Remove from freezer and place on countertop to thaw before use. May reheat in the oven on a half-sheet pan uncovered. May be frozen up to 1 month.

Your Notes:

_____

_____

Basmati Rice

Ingredients:
2 cup Basmati rice

rinsing water

4 cups water

1 tsp salt

Directions:
Step 1:

In a bowl, add rice and fresh, room temperature water, enough to cover the rice. Swirl your hand through the water and the rice, until the water is cloudy. That is the excess starch leaving the rice.

Step 2:

Drain out the water.

Step 3:

Repeat Steps 1 & 2, until you can swirl your hand without making it cloudy. Drain water. Set aside.

Step 4:

In a pot, on high heat, add water and salt, bring to a boil.

Step 5:
Add rice, then stir and allow water to boil again.

Step 6:
Reduce heat to low and cover the pot with a lid. Allow to cook for 15 minutes.

Step 7:
Transfer pot to a heat-safe surface such as a cold stovetop burner. Allow to sit for 5 minutes.

Step 8:
Remove the lid, then gently fluff rice with a fork.

Fresh Storage:
Cover with plastic wrap / film and store in the refrigerator. Reheat in a pot with a splash of water. Use within 1 week.

Frozen Storage:
Do NOT freeze.

Your Notes:

Tortillas

Ingredients:
2 cups flour

1/2 tsp salt

1/2 tsp baking powder

1/8 cup butter, softened

1/8 cup lard or solid vegetable shortening / "Crisco"

3/4 cup warm water (80 - 100 degrees)

Directions:
Step 1:

In a bowl, add flour, salt, baking powder, butter, and shortening.

Step 2:

With bare hands, coat the shortening and butter a little bit with dry mixture, then begin breaking up shortening and butter with a motion similar to snapping your fingers with your thumb moving across all fingers, while you mix the shortening and butter more with the dry mixture, until the dough is mealy and gritty in appearance and texture (no pieces bigger than pea-sized). Rub hands together to remove any mix that sticks to them.

Step 3:
Add water, then stir, to mix well.

Step 4:
Dough should be slightly moist but not very sticky. If dough is too dry, add 1 tsp of water, then mix. Repeat this additional water and mixing, until the dough is correct. Set aside.

Step 5:
Sprinkle flour onto a flat, clean, dry work surface.

Step 6:
Transfer dough to countertop. Cut dough in half.

Step 7:
Cut each half into half again.

Step 8:
Cut each quarter in half again, for a total of 8 pieces of dough. Set aside.

Step 9:
Preheat a dry pan on medium heat.

Step 10:
Set out a dinner-size plate or serving platter. Wet a clean dish- / kitchen-towel with warm tap water, wring it out, then place it over the plate / platter.

Step 11:
With 1 piece of dough, cup your bare hand over the top of the dough, then roll it around in tight circles on the countertop, to shape it into a smooth and round ball. Set aside.

Step 12:
Repeat Step 11, until remaining pieces have been made into balls.

Step 13:
On the floured work surface, add 1 dough ball, then using a rolling pin, press down and roll out from the center of the dough ball, over and over, each time rolling in a different direction, until you roll out an 8" circle of even thickness.

Step 14:
Lightly spritz hot pan with non-stick cooking vegetable oil spray.

Step 15:
Transfer 1 dough circle to the pan, gently lowering it on 1 edge and then laying dough down flat.

Step 16:
Fry for 1 minute. You will see the dough begin to bubble, this is a good sign.

Step 17:
Using tongs, grasp 1 edge and flip over the dough circle. Fry 1 more minute.

Step 18:
Then, using tongs, grasp 1 edge, hold the fry bread above the pan to allow oil to drain for a few seconds, and then stack on a dinner-size plate or serving platter, covering the tortilla with the warm, damp towel. Set aside.

Step 19:
Repeat Steps 13 - 18, until all tortillas have been made.

Fresh Storage:

Once cooled to room temperature, cover the tortillas with plastic wrap / film and store in the refrigerator. May reheat in the microwave if spritzed with plain water to avoid over-drying. Use within 1 week.

Frozen Storage:

Do NOT freeze.

Your Notes:

Movie Inspired Meals

Recipes List:

147 Movie Five:
Broccoli Salad
Chicken Marsala
English Trifle

170 Movie Six:
Couscous Salad
Greek Meatballs in Sauce
Plum & Almond Crumble

184 Movie Seven:
Red & White Bites
Black & Blue Mussels served with
    Herbed Gnocchi
Gold & Amber Bread Pudding served with
    Pecan Sauce

201 Movie Eight:
Italian Salad served with Italian Dressing
Spaghetti & Meatballs served with
    Marinara Sauce & with Garlic Bread
Zabaglione

218 Movie Nine:
Tortilla Soup
Fish Tacos served with Mango & Banana Salsa
Apricot Flan

236 Movie Ten:
Olive Tapenade served on Crostini
Timpano
Strawberry Ice Cream

253 Movie Eleven:
Cucumber Salad
Beef Bourguignon
Italian Crème Cake with
　　　Italian Buttercream Frosting

275 Movie Twelve:
Chorizo Stuffed Poblano Peppers
Moqueca de Camarão
　　　aka Brazilian Shrimp Stew
Orange Flan

288 Movie Thirteen:
Wild Rice & Mushrooms
Baked Walleye served with Caramelized Carrots
Fry Bread

303 Movie Fourteen:
Black-Eyed Peas Relish Crudité
BBQ Beef Brisket
Browned Butter Carrot Cake with
　　　Cream Cheese Frosting

325 Movie Fifteen:

Cornbread served with Bacon & Shrimp & Creole Remoulade

Salmon served with Lemon Crème Fraiche Sauce

Blackberry & Peach Cream Crumble

346 Movie Sixteen:

Caprese Bites

Sausage and Peppers served with Pasta

Plum Grappa Granita

356 Movie Seventeen:

Gallo Pinto

Puerco Pibil

Aztec Éclair Puffs

373 Movie Eighteen:

Prosciutto Pears

Mushroom Ravioli

Panna Cotta with Fresh Berries

387 Movie Nineteen:

Grapefruit Salad,

Lamb Stew with Dried Plums

Cinnamon Mouse with Orange Segments

402 Movie Twenty:

Fried Green Tomatoes served with Dipping
   Sauce

Pork Chops served with Greens in a Cherries &
   Port Wine Reduction

Bourbon Pecan Tart

422 Movie Twenty-One:

Hoppin John

Shrimp Sunset Sauté served with Angel Hair
   Pasta

Beignets

436 Movie Twenty-Two:

Duck Hash served on Toasted Baguette

Sea Scallops served with Asparagus &
   Tangerine Sauce

Crème Brûlée with Orange

454 Movie Twenty-Three:

Pepperoncini Bites

Chicken Salad with Goat Cheese served with
   Balsamic Vinaigrette Dressing

Tiramisu

471 Movie Twenty-Four:
Spaghetti Squash Fritters
Brazilian Pan-Seared Steak served with
    Wild Mushroom Ragoût
Blueberry "Caviar" served with Baked Brie

484 Movie Twenty-Five:
Spring Rolls served with Peanut-Hoisin Sauce
Chinese-BBQ Pork
New Year Cookies

500 Movie Twenty-Six:
Veggie Antipasti Zucchini Boats
Pizza Napoletana
White Russian Pie

524 Movie Twenty-Seven:
Mushroom Soup
Shepherd's Pie
Chocolate Digestive Biscuit with Builder's Tea

540 Movie Twenty-Eight:
Cucumber & Goat Cheese Bites
Ratatouille
Chocolate Cake with Chocolate Frosting

559 Movie Twenty-Nine:
Frisée Salad with Lardons & Poached Eggs
Salmon in Basil Sauce served with Lemon
Couscous
Chocolate Pots de Crème

574 Movie Thirty:
Deviled Bacon Eggs
Korean BBQ Lettuce Cups
Red Velvet Cupcakes

Movie Inspired Meals

Recipes &

MIM Trivia Game

Peace and Bon Appétit: James and Lisa

MOVIE ONE

Course #1: Plantain Chips and Mango Salsa

Mango Salsa Ingredients:

1 mango, peeled and diced 1/4" cubes

1/2 cup cucumber, peeled and diced 1/4" cubes

1 jalapeño, seeded and minced

1/3 cup red onion, diced 1/8"

1 Tbsp lime juice

1/3 cup cilantro, stemmed and chopped roughly

Mango Salsa Directions:

Step 1:

In a bowl, add mango, cucumber, jalapeño, red onion, lime juice, and cilantro, then stir to mix well.

Step 2:

Cover with plastic wrap / film.

Step 3:

Transfer to refrigerator for 1 hour before use.

Fresh Storage:

Cover the salsa bowl with plastic wrap / film or place salsa in a plastic sealable bag and store in the refrigerator. Use within 5 days.

Frozen Storage:

Do NOT freeze.

Your Notes:

_____

Plantain Chips Ingredients:

vegetable oil (for frying)
2 green plantains, peeled and sliced 1/8" ovals
2 limes, zested and juiced
salt, to taste

Plantain Chips Directions:

Step 1:
Place several sheets of paper towel or paper bags on a plate. Set aside.

Step 2:
Add vegetable oil in a deep pan (preferably cast iron), until 1" deep.

Step 3:
Preheat pan, medium-high heat, until oil is 350 degrees.

Step 4:
Carefully and slowly transfer only enough plantains to make 1 layer deep in the oil, then fry for 1 minute.

Step 5:
Transfer fried plantain chips to the towel/bag-lined plate to drain oil.

Step 6:
Flip the chips over to drain off the other side. Set aside.

Step 7:
Repeat Steps 4 – 6, until all plantain chips are made.

Step 8:
Sprinkle to add lime zest, lime juice, and salt, to taste.

Step 9:
Serve immediately with Mango Salsa for dipping.

Fresh Storage:
Do not store.

Frozen Storage:
Do not freeze.

Your Notes:

MOVIE ONE

Course #2: Mayan Cocoa Chicken Mole served with Tortillas

Tortillas: Frequently Used Side Item Recipes

Mayan Cocoa Chicken Mole Ingredients:

2 Tbsp peanut oil

5 lbs skinless, boneless chicken thighs

3 cups chicken stock / broth

2 cups orange juice

2 Tbsp peanut oil

2 cups yellow onions, peeled and diced 1/8"

1/2 cup almonds, sliced thinly

6 large garlic cloves, peeled, smashed, and sliced thinly

4 tsp cumin seeds

4 tsp coriander seeds

15 dried pasilla chiles, stemmed, seeded, torn into 1"
    pieces, and rinsed

3 dried ancho chiles, stemmed, seeded, torn into 1"
    pieces, and rinsed

3 dried mulato chiles, stemmed, seeded, torn into 1"
    pieces, and rinsed

1/4 cup raisins

zest of 1 small orange

1 & 1/2 tsp dried oregano

1 disk Taza Guajillo Chili Chocolate Mexicano

1/4 tsp cinnamon

1 bunch cilantro, stemmed and chopped

Mayan Cocoa Chicken Mole Directions:
Step 1:

To raw chicken, add salt and pepper, to taste, to both sides. Set aside.

Step 2:

In a pot, on medium-high heat, add 2 Tbsp oil and enough chicken pieces until have just 1 layer of chicken in the pot, then cook, until lightly browned.

Step 3:

Transfer browned chicken pieces to a bowl. Set aside.

Step 4:

Repeat Steps 2 & 3, until all chicken is browned.

Step 5:
Reduce pot heat to medium-low. Transfer browned chicken and any juices to pot.

Step 6:
Add stock and orange juice. Cover and simmer (almost boiling but not at full boil) for 20 minutes.

Step 7:
While chicken simmers... In a pan, on medium-high heat, add other 2 Tbsp oil and onions, then sauté 15 minutes, until golden-brown colored.

Step 8:
Reduce onion pan to medium heat. Add almonds, cumin, and coriander, then sauté 2 minutes, until nuts begin to color and spices become fragrant.

Step 9:
Add chiles and garlic, then stir. Cook 3 minutes, stirring occasionally, until chiles begin to soften.

Step 10:
Transfer simmered chicken into a bowl, leaving the liquid in the pot. Set bowl aside.

Step 11:
Transfer remaining liquid into onion pan. Set empty pot aside.

Step 12:
To pan, add raisins, orange zest, and oregano, then cover and simmer (almost boiling but not at full boil) 30 minutes, until chilies are very soft.

Step 13:
Transfer pan to a heat-safe surface, such as a cold stovetop burner.

Step 14:
Add chocolate and cinnamon, then let mixture stand 15 minutes, until chocolate melts and mixture cools slightly.

Step 15:
In a blender or food processor, add sauce mixture, being careful not to add more than 1/4 of total volume space available in the container, then puree, until smooth. (Danger! Using too much hot liquid at a time can result in splattering with serious burn risk!)

Step 16:
Transfer puree into the reserved empty chicken pot.

Step 17:
Repeat Steps 15 & 16, until all sauce is pureed.

Step 18:
To sauce, add salt and pepper, to taste. Set aside.

Step 19:
Transfer chicken to a cutting board, then using 2 total forks, place 1 fork in each hand. Use the 1 fork to hold the chicken in place, then use the other fork to scrape away layers of chicken in strands, making all pieces into shredded chicken. Set aside.

Step 20:
Add chicken to sauce.

Step 21:
Sprinkle to add cilantro.

Step 22:
Serve chicken in mole sauce with warm tortillas.

Fresh Storage:

Once cooled to room temperature, cover the chicken in the sauce with plastic wrap / film and store in the refrigerator. Reheat in a pan. Use within 3 days.

Frozen Storage:

Once cooled to room temperature, cover the chicken with plastic wrap / film, move to refrigerator until completely cooled, then move to freezer. Remove from freezer and transfer to refrigerator to thaw before use. Reheat in a pan. May be frozen up to 1 month.

Your Notes:

_____

_____

MOVIE ONE

Course #3: Caramelized Pears in Puff Pastry

Ingredients:

2 pears peeled, seeded, and halved (any varietal)

1/2 cup sugar

1/4 cup cool tap water

2 Tbsp butter

1 tsp lemon juice

1 tsp vanilla extract

1 sheet puff pastry (from frozen section at store)

1 Tbsp butter, melted

2 Tbsp sugar

4 scoops vanilla ice cream (your favorite brand and type)

Directions:

Step 1:

Preheat oven to 350 degrees.

Step 2:
Place pears flat-side down on the countertop, close together but not touching.

Step 3:
Drape one puff pastry sheet over all four pear halves.

Step 4:
Using bare hands, gently form the sheet into a cover or "shell" over each pear half.

Step 5:
Use a knife to trim each one along the edges of the pears.

Step 6:
Remove the pastry shells from the pear halves and set pastry shells aside.

Step 7:
In a non-stick pan, on medium-high heat, add sugar and water, then stir to mix well.

Step 8:
Heat until the sugar begins to turn medium-amber colored.

Step 9:
Add butter, lemon juice, and vanilla extract, then stir to mix well.

Step 10:
Add pear halves with the flat-side down, and reduce to medium heat. Cook for 3 minutes.

Step 11:
Transfer the pear halves to a baking sheet, placing flat-side down.

Step 12:
Transfer the pan with the remaining mixture to a heat-safe surface, such as a cold stovetop burner, and set aside.

Step 13:
Cover the pear halves with the pre-formed puff pastry shells.

Step 14:
Brush the outside of the shells with the melted butter mixture.

Step 15:
Sprinkle to add 2 Tbsp sugar.

Step 16:
Set remaining butter mixture aside on a heat-safe surface, such as a cold stovetop burner.

Step 17:
Place the baking sheet into the preheated oven, on the middle rack. Bake for approximately 15 minutes, until pastry shells are golden-brown.

Step 18:
Using a heat-safe spatula, transfer pastry-side-down onto serving plates or bowls.

Step 19:
Drizzle butter mixture over each one, then add a scoop
of ice cream next to each one.

Fresh Storage:
Do not store.

Frozen Storage:
Do not freeze.

Your Notes:

_____

_____

Round One Guess As to the Inspirational Movie:

_____

MOVIE ONE

Level One Hint:

- The inspired dish was served to a supporting female focal character for her birthday, after which she died.

Round Two Guess As to the Inspirational Movie:

MOVIE ONE

Level Two Hints:

- The female protagonist and her daughter move with the wind, just like her mother did with her.

- An American-British film from 2000, based upon a novel with the same name, set in France in 1959.

- Nominated for 5 Academy Awards, including Best Picture. Winner of Best Actress for European Film Awards and of Best Supporting Actress for Screen Actors Guild.

- A kangaroo named Pantouffe hops unseen yet still requests stories and asks questions.

Round Three Guess As to the Inspirational Movie:

MOVIE ONE

Level Three Hints:

- Mayan Cocoa Chicken Mole served with Tortillas
- He was on screen in this as "Roux", a "river rat", three years before he appeared as "Captain Jack Sparrow" the pirate.
- What did you see in the wheel that Vianne spins for her customers?
- Carrie-Anne Moss is "Caroline Clairmont", who works in the Comte de Reynaud's office and is the daughter of Armande Voizin, played by Judi Dench. Demure "Caroline Clairmont" is a far cry from Moss' previous role as "Trinity" in The Matrix, released just the year before.

Round Four Guess As to the Inspirational Movie:

MOVIE TWO

Course #1: Dosas served with Potato Masala

Dosas Ingredients:

3/4 cup Idli rice

3 cups water

1/4 cup Urad dal

1/8 tsp fenugreek seeds

1 cup water

1/8 cup leftover Basmati or other cooked rice

1 cup water

1/2 tsp salt

Dosas Directions:

Step 1:

In a bowl, add Idli rice and 3 cups of water. Set aside for 4 hours. After 1 hour, do Step 2.

Step 2:

In another bowl, add Urad dal, fenugreek seeds, and 1 cup of water. Set aside for 3 hours.

Step 3:

Drain Urad dal bowl water into another bowl to keep the soaking water in reserve.

Step 4:

In a blender, add 1/4 cup of the Udal dal water reserved and all of the Urad dal drained mix. Blend until smooth and light.

Step 5:

Add more of the reserved water as necessary to get to the smooth consistency; may take up to 1/4 to 1/2 cup.

Step 6:

Transfer to a bowl. Set aside.

Step 7:

In a blender, add the drained Idli rice, the leftover cooked rice, and 1/2 cup Udal dal reserved water. Blend until smooth and creamy.

Step 8:
If needed to make smooth and creamy, then add from 1/8 to 1/2 cup more Udal dal reserved water.

Step 9:
In a bowl, mix the Urad dal mix and the Idli rice mix.

Step 10:
Add salt, to taste.

Step 11:
Set aside, at room temperature, to rise for 9 hours.

Step 12:
Batter may be covered and refrigerated up to 2 days. Or set aside to use immediately in Potato Masala Directions Step 8 to make into Dosas.

Potato Masala Ingredients:
2 cup potatoes (any varietal), diced 1/4"
3 Tbsp salt
2 Tbsp vegetable oil
1/4 cup white or yellow onion, diced 1/4"
1/2 tsp cumin seeds

1/2 tsp mustard seeds

1/2 tsp turmeric

1 green chili, seeded and minced

1/2 tsp salt

1 tsp lemon juice

1 Tbsp cilantro, washed well, stemmed, and chopped

Potato Masala Directions:

Step 1:

In a pot, add 4 qts tap water, potatoes, and 3 Tbsp salt.
Boil on high heat.

Step 2:

Potatoes are done when you can insert a fork upside
down into a potato piece, lift the potato piece above the
water level, and the piece slides off of the fork.

Step 3:

Drain the water, then move the pot to a heat-safe
surface, such as a cool stove burner, and allow to cool at
least 30 minutes, until room temperature.

Step 4:

In a pan, on medium-high heat, add oil, onion, cumin, and mustard seeds.

Step 5:

Once you hear the seeds pop and crack, add turmeric, chili pepper, salt, and cooled potatoes, then stir to mix well. Cook for 5 minutes.

Step 6:

Remove from heat, add lemon juice and cilantro. Set aside on a heat-safe surface.

Step 7:

In a non-stick pan, lightly coat with nonstick vegetable cooking oil spray, and set to medium heat.

Step 8:

Retrieve Dosa batter from previous recipe preparation.

Step 9:
Using a ladle or large serving spoon, pour batter slowly and in a circular pattern to make a filled circle, similar to a crepe or tortilla thickness, making sure that the thickness is fairly even.

Step 10:
Fry dosa for 1 minute, then using a spatula, gently lift an edge to check the underside for a golden-brown color.

Step 11:
Once color is achieved, using a spatula, flip dosa.

Step 12:
Fry dosa for 1 minute, then using a spatula, gently life an edge to check the underside for a golden-brown color.

Step 13:
Once color is achieved, using a spatula, transfer the dosa to a serving platter and set aside.

Step 14:

Repeat Steps 9 - 13, until all batter has been made into dosas, making sure to recoat pan with cooking oil spray for each repeat process.

Step 15:

For each dosa, place potato masala in the center and either fold in half, like a taco.

Fresh Storage:

Once cooled to room temperature, cover the potato masala with plastic wrap / film and store in the refrigerator. Reheat in a pan. Use within 4 days.
Once cooled to room temperature, cover the fried dosas with plastic wrap / film and store in the refrigerator. Reheat in a pan lightly coated with vegetable cooking oil spray. Use within 2 days.

Frozen Storage:

Do not freeze dosas or potato masala.

Your Notes:

_____

MOVIE TWO

Course #2: Saag Paneer

Ingredients:

1 tsp turmeric

1/2 tsp cayenne

1 tsp salt

2 oz vegetable oil

12 oz paneer, cut 1/2" cubes

16 oz frozen chopped spinach, thawed

1/2 cup white onion, minced

1 Tbsp ginger, minced

1 Tbsp garlic, minced

1 Serrano chili, seeded and minced

1/2 tsp Garam Masala (a prepared powdered spice)

2 & 1/2 tsp ground cumin

1/4 cup vegetable broth / stock

1/2 cup plain Greek yogurt (or dairy or soy)

Directions:

Step 1:

In a bowl, add turmeric, cayenne, salt, and oil, then stir to mix well.

Step 2:

Add paneer cubes and toss to coat with spiced oil. Set aside.

Step 3:

On a cutting board, finely chop spinach. Set aside.

Step 4:

In a pan, on medium heat, add coated paneer, then turn cubes over frequently until browned on at least two sides.

Step 5:

Transfer paneer to a bowl and set aside. Put empty pan back on the medium heat burner.

Step 6:

To the still hot pan, add onions, ginger, garlic, and chili, then stir to mix well. Sauté for 12 minutes, constantly moving contents in the pan by either gently moving pan forward and backward then occasionally flipping the contents over, all while holding the pan's handle, or by gently stirring with a spatula / spoon.

(Note: The contents should not dry out, so if the contents quit releasing liquid and start looking dry, then add a little tap water at a time to avoid burning contents.)

Step 7:

Add garam masala, cumin, vegetable broth /stock, then stir to mix well. Cook for 5 minutes.

Step 8:

Turn heat to low. Add yogurt, then stir to mix well.

Step 9:

Add paneer, then heat through.

Fresh Storage:

Once cooled to room temperature, cover the saag paneer with plastic wrap / film and store in the refrigerator. Reheat in a pan. Use within 3 days.

Frozen Storage:

Do not freeze.

Your Notes:

_____

_____

MOVIE TWO

Course #3: Melon Soup

Ingredients:

4 cups honeydew melon, rind removed and seeded, 1/4 – 1/2" cubed

1/2 cup plain Greek yogurt (or dairy or soy)

1 Tbsp sugar

1 Tbsp honey

1 Tbsp ginger, minced

4 mint leaves, stemmed

1/4 tsp salt

1/8 tsp ground black pepper

1 Tbsp lemon juice

Directions:

Step 1:

In a blender or food processor, add melon, yogurt, sugar, honey, ginger, mint, salt, pepper, and lemon juice, then puree until smooth.

Step 2:
Transfer to a bowl. Cover with plastic wrap/film.

Step 3:
Transfer to refrigerator to chill at least 30 minutes.

Fresh Storage:
Cover bowl with plastic wrap / film and store in the refrigerator. Use within 3 days.

Frozen Storage:
Do not freeze.

Your Notes:

_____

_____

Round One Guess As to the Inspirational Movie:

_____

MOVIE TWO

Level One Hint:

- The inspired dish is offered for free by the protagonist's father in the family's restaurant, "Tandoori Palace", trying to encourage people to become customers for the struggling business.

Round Two Guess As to the Inspirational Movie:

MOVIE TWO

Level Two Hints:

- A cab-driving focal character influences the protagonist to embrace his Indian cuisine heritage with a discussion of how he makes a dish that will you would remember like you remember a lost love.

- A trip through a local market leads to unique and memorable descriptions of spices.

- In a moment of frustration, Sous Chef Samir tells Carrie to get her hair pulled up so that out of her face, as he can find no fault with her cooking.

- The inspirational movie opens with a visual montage of dough, cheese, spinach, and meats, then a restaurant kitchen with people yelling about lobster fennel and filleting salmon.

Round Three Guess As to the Inspirational Movie:

_____

MOVIE TWO

Level Three Hints:

- Dosa served with Potato Masala
- The Sous Chef is told by his Chef that another person was chosen over him, due to Sous' cooking being cold whereas the other person's cooking is magic and gives the Chef a "boner".
- The "uncles" help find the mysterious cab-driving focal character, Akbar, with their contacts within the Indian immigrant community of cab drivers.
- Among the "uncles", there is a lively discussion of the 3 passions in a man's life: country, religion, and cricket, which is accompanied by a comment about how a wife fits in to a man's life.
- When Samir learns to trust his instincts and senses rather than cook from recipes, he becomes a Chef and revitalizes the family restaurant.

Round Four Guess As to the Inspirational Movie:

MOVIE THREE

Course #1: Garlic Naan with Cilantro Pesto

Garlic Naan Ingredients:

4 cups flour

1 tsp baking powder

1 tsp salt

2 tsp garlic powder

2 cups plain Greek yogurt (or dairy or soy)

Garlic Naan Directions:

Step 1:

In a bowl, add flour, baking powder, garlic powder, and salt, then stir with a spoon / spatula to mix well.

Step 2:

Add yogurt, the stir with a spoon / spatula to mix well.

Step 3:
Knead 3 to 4 minutes, until smooth and pliable. **Or** put in an electric mixer with dough hook attachment and mix in the bowl for 3 to 4 minutes on low speed, only adding a little extra flour if sticky.

Step 4:
Sprinkle flour onto a flat, clean, dry work surface.

Step 5:
Divide dough into 10 equal pieces. Set aside.

Step 6:
Preheat a dry pan or griddle on medium heat.

Step 7:
Set out a dinner-size plate or serving platter. Wet a clean dish-/kitchen-towel with warm tap water, wring it out, then place it over the plate/platter.

Step 8:
Retrieve 1 piece of dough. Cup your hand over the top of the dough, then roll it around in tight circles on the countertop, to shape it into a smooth and round ball. Set aside.

Step 9:
Repeat Step 8, until remaining pieces are shaped.

Step 10:
On the floured work surface, using a rolling pin, press down and roll out from the center of the dough ball, over and over, each time rolling in a different direction, until you roll out an 8" circle of even thickness.

Step 11:
Lightly spritz hot pan with non-stick cooking vegetable oil spray.

Step 12:
Transfer 1 dough circle to the pan, gently lowering it on 1 edge and then laying dough down flat.

Step 13:

Fry for 1 to 2 minutes. The naan will puff up and develop brown spots.

Step 14:

Using tongs, grasp 1 edge and flip over the dough circle.

Step 15:

Fry 1 to 2 more minutes, until lightly-brown colored.

Step 16:

Then, using tongs, grasp 1 edge, hold the naan above the pan to allow oil to drain for a few seconds, and then stack on a plain plate or serving platter, covering the naan with the warm, damp towel. Set aside.

Step 17:

Repeat Steps 11 – 16, until remaining naan have been made.

Step 18:

Cover naan with the warm, damp towel, until ready to serve.

Fresh Storage:

Once cooled to room temperature, cover naan with plastic wrap / film or place in a plastic sealable bag and store in the refrigerator. May reheat in the oven if wrapped entirely in aluminum foil (just one or in a stack) or in a microwave uncovered. Use within 1 week.

Frozen Storage:

Once cooled to room temperature, cover naan with plastic wrap / film or place in a plastic sealable bag, move to refrigerator until completely cooled, then move to freezer. Remove from freezer and place on countertop to thaw before use. May reheat in the oven if wrapped entirely in aluminum foil (just one or in a stack) or in a microwave uncovered. May be frozen up to 1 month.

Your Notes:

_____

_____

Cilantro Pesto Ingredients:

1 cup cilantro leaves, well rinsed under cold running water and coarsely chopped

2 tsp garlic, minced

1/8 cup toasted cashews

1/3 cup parmesan, finely grated

1/4 tsp salt

1/2 cup peanut oil

Cilantro Pesto Directions:

Step 1:

In a blender or food processor, add cilantro, garlic, cashews, parmesan, and salt. Blend until smooth and creamy.

Step 2:

With blender running on medium, slowly drizzle in oil, until well mixed with rest of ingredients.

Step 3:

Add additional salt, to taste.

Step 4:

Serve with naan as spread or for dipping.

Fresh Storage:

Cover the cilantro pesto with plastic wrap / film or place in a plastic sealable bag and store in the refrigerator. Use within 3 days.

Frozen Storage:

Cover the cilantro pesto with plastic wrap / film or place in a plastic sealable bag, and store in freezer. Remove from freezer and place on countertop to thaw before use. May be frozen up to 1 month.

Your Notes:

_____

_____

MOVIE THREE

Course #2: Butter Chicken served over Basmati Rice

Basmati Rice: Frequently Used Side Item Recipes

Marinated Chicken Ingredients:

1 cup Greek yogurt (or dairy or soy)

1 Tbsp ginger, minced

1 Tbsp garlic, minced

2 Tbsp Garam Masala

1/4 cup canned tomato puree

1/4 tsp salt

2 Tbsp lemon juice

2 Tbsp butter, melted

4 boneless, skinless chicken breasts, score 1/2" deep
      cuts spaced about 1" apart (in any one direction)

Marinated Chicken Directions:

Step 1:

In a bowl, add yogurt, ginger, garlic, Garam Masala, tomato puree, salt, lemon juice, and butter, then stir to mix well.

Step 2:

Add chicken, stir well.

Step 3:

Cover with plastic wrap / film. Transfer to refrigerator to chill for 1 hour.

Step 4:

Preheat oven to 400 degrees.

Step 5:

Transfer chicken to a roasting pan.

Step 6:

Pour remaining marinade over chicken.

Step 7:
Place the roasting pan into the preheated oven, on the middle rack. Bake for 25 minutes, until internal temperature is at least 180 degrees on your thermometer.

Step 8:
Remove pan from the oven and place on a heat safe surface such as your stovetop. Set aside, then make the sauce.

Sauce Ingredients:
4 Tbsp butter
1 Tbsp ginger, minced
1 Tbsp garlic, minced
14.5 oz can diced tomato, drained
1 Serrano chili, seeded and finely minced
1 cup dairy heavy whipping cream
salt, to taste

Sauce Directions:
Step 1:
In a pan, on medium heat, add butter, ginger, and garlic, then stir to mix well. Cook 1 minute, until aromatic.

Step 2:
Add tomatoes, chili pepper, cooked chicken, and chicken marinade, then stir to mix well. Cook for 10 minutes.

Step 3:
Add heavy cream, then stir to mix well.

Step 4:
Add salt, to taste.

Step 5:
Serve Butter Chicken over Basmati Rice.

Fresh Storage:
Cover finished butter chicken dish with plastic wrap / film or place in a plastic sealable bag and store in the refrigerator. Reheat in a pan. Use within 3 days.

Frozen Storage:

Cover finished butter chicken dish with plastic wrap / film or place in a plastic sealable bag, and store in freezer. Remove from freezer and transfer to refrigerator to thaw before use. Reheat in a pan. May be frozen up to 2 weeks.

Your Notes:

_____

_____

MOVIE THREE

Course #3: Lime & Ginger Cookies

Ingredients:

1 & 1/2 cup sugar

2 Tbsp lime zest

1 Tbsp fresh ginger, peeled and minced

14 Tbsp butter, cut into chunks and slightly softened

1 egg, separated and yolk kept

1 & 1/2 Tbsp lime juice

3 tsp ground ginger powder

1/2 tsp vanilla extract

1/2 tsp baking soda

1/4 tsp salt

2 & 1/4 cups flour

parchment paper to line cookie sheets

Directions:

Step 1:

Preheat oven to 350 degrees.

Step 2:
In a food processor, blender, coffee grinder, or spice grinder, add sugar, lime zest, and minced ginger, then process for several minutes, until mixed well and juice from ginger has made the mixture into a crumbly paste texture.

Step 3:
Remove 1/3 cup and transfer to a plate and set aside, then transfer remaining mixture to a bowl for mixing.

Step 4:
To the mixing bowl, add butter, yolk, lime juice, ginger powder, vanilla extract, baking soda, and salt, then with a handheld or stand electric mixer, medium speed, beat to mix well.

Step 5:
Reduce mixing speed to low, add flour a little at a time, scraping the bowl, until mixed well. Dough will be a little sticky but will be soft and moldable into shapes.

Step 6:

On a flat, clean, dry work surface OR with clean, dry hands, with hands or with a rolling pin, press down and roll out from the center of the dough ball, over and over, each time rolling in a different direction, until you roll out a rough square about 1/4" thick and even thickness.

Step 7:

Using a knife or dough cutter, cut the square into 4 equal squares.

Step 8:

Cut each square into 4 strips horizontally and into 4 strips vertically, creating 16 square pieces out of each of the 4 squares.

Step 9:

Using the palm of your hand, take 1 small piece and gently roll it around on a hard surface or in the palm of your other hand, until it forms a ball shape.

Step 10:

Gently roll that ball shape in the set aside mixture on the plate from Step 3, until lightly coated.

Step 11:
Transfer the ball to a parchment lined cookie sheet.

Step 12:
Using a glass measuring cup or other heavy glass, center the glass over the ball shape, then press down until the ball is flattened and about 1/4" thick.

Step 13:
Repeat Steps 9 - 12 for all remaining pieces, leaving 1" of space between the 1/4" flattened cookies.

Step 14:
Place cookie sheet into the preheated oven, on the middle rack. Bake for 13-15 minutes, until the edges are starting to get firm and a light golden-brown color.

Step 15:
Remove cookie sheet and place on a heat-safe surface, such as your cold stovetop.

Step 16:
Using a spatula, transfer cookies to a wire rack to cool for 5 minutes.

Step 17:
Serve alone or with vanilla bean ice cream.

Fresh Storage:

Allow cookies to cool completely, then cover cookies with plastic wrap / film or place in a plastic sealable bag and store at room temperature. Use within 3 days. Do NOT refrigerate.

Frozen Storage:

Allow cookies to cool completely, then place in a plastic sealable bag or container, and store in freezer. Remove from freezer and place on countertop to thaw before use. May be frozen up to 2 months.

Your Notes:

_____

Round One Guess As to the Inspirational Movie:

_____

MOVIE THREE

Level One Hint:

- This classic, inspired dish is being taught on a television cooking show while the Chef protagonist is cuddled up with his wife on the sofa discussing their servant cook not wanting to be his guru.

Round Two Guess As to the Inspirational Movie:

_____

MOVIE THREE

Level Two Hints:

- The female antagonist learned to cook from her grandmother and has been cooking for and stealing from households for 30 years.
- The servant cook tells the protagonist Chef how to cook fenugreek.
- Mustard seed is often shown during cooking scenes as well as for making healing oil to massage on the sick baby's stomach.
- The protagonist is asked to give cooking lessons to the wives of the diplomats but makes the cultural mistake of using beef.

Round Three Guess As to the Inspirational Movie:

_____

MOVIE THREE

Level Three Hints:

- Butter Chicken served over Basmati Rice
- This inspirational movie was based upon a true story full of satirical wit showing social exaggerations of the two cultures.
- The Canadian protagonist and his diplomat wife live in the embassy compound for safety but end up being conned at every turn by the Indian servants and their cohorts.

Round Four Guess As to the Inspirational Movie:

MOVIE FOUR

Course #1: Braised Bean Curd, Spinach, & Mushrooms served with Basmati Rice

Basmati Rice: Frequently Used Side Item Recipes

Ingredients:
3 Tbsp vegetable oil

1/2 tsp fresh ginger, minced

1 block tofu (firm or extra firm), pressed and cut into 1" cubes

3 cups Buna-Shimeji mushrooms (or button white mushrooms)

1 chili pepper, seeded and minced

2 tsp oyster sauce

2 tsp San-G soya sauce

1 tsp brown sugar

2 cups fresh spinach, chopped

Directions:

Step 1:

In a pan, on high heat, add oil.

Step 2:

Add ginger, then cook for 10 seconds.

Step 3:

Add tofu, then stir to mix well. Cook for 3 minutes, until light golden-brown colored.

Step 4:

Add mushrooms and chili, then stir to mix well. Cook for 3 minutes.

Step 5:

Add oyster sauce, San-G, and sugar, then stir to mix well. Cook for 2 minutes.

Step 6:

Drop in spinach, then cook until wilted.

Step 7:

Spoon over rice or serve beside rice.

Fresh Storage:

Cover with plastic wrap / film or place in a plastic sealable bag and store in the refrigerator. Reheat in a pan. Use within 3 days.

Frozen Storage:

Do NOT freeze.

Your Notes:

_____

_____

MOVIE FOUR

Course #2: Peking Duck Pancakes

Duck Ingredients:
2 Tbsp Hoisin sauce
1 & 1/2 tsp garlic, minced
1/4 tsp Chinese Five Spice powder
1 Tbsp San-G soya sauce
1/2 Tbsp sugar
1 tsp rice wine vinegar (plain, not sweet)
1 Tbsp Chinese rice wine (not a cooking wine – found in
    cooking sauces section)
4 duck breasts, skin intact

Duck Directions:
Step 1:
In a bowl, add Hoisin, garlic, Chinese Five Spice
powder, San-G, sugar, rice wine vinegar, and rice wine,
then stir well. Set aside.

Step 2:
Score duck breast with a knife in a series of cuts about 1/2" apart going through the fat but not reaching the meat.

Step 3:
Turn duck breast 90 degrees and cut another set of lines to make a diamond pattern.

Step 4:
Transfer duck to bowl of sauce, then toss the meat to coat it in sauce.

Step 5:
Cover the bowl with plastic wrap / film.

Step 6:
Transfer to refrigerator, then chill for 3 hours. Use within 1 day.

Scallion Pancakes Ingredients:

1 & 1/2 cups flour

1 & 1/4 tsp salt

3 scallions, green parts only, sliced thinly

1/2 cup water

peanut oil

1/3 cup Hoisin sauce

Scallion Pancakes Directions:

Step 1:

In a bowl, add flour, salt, and scallions, then stir well. Set aside.

Step 2:

In a pot, on high heat, add water, then bring to boil.

Step 3:

Add hot water to flour mixture, then stir well to make a dough.

Step 4:

Knead dough for 6 minutes.

Step 5:
Transfer the dough to a clean bowl and cover with plastic wrap / film.

Step 6:
Set aside for 30 minutes at room temperature or up to 1 day in the refrigerator.

Combined Peking Duck Pancakes Dish Directions:
Step 1:
Preheat oven to 425 degrees.

Step 2:
In an oven-safe pan, medium high heat, add duck breasts fat-side down, then cook about 7 minutes, until the skin looks crispy and is deep golden-brown colored.

Step 3:
Using tongs or a spatula, turn duck breasts over.

Step 4:
Transfer pan to the preheated oven, on the middle rack. Bake for 7 minutes.

Step 5:

Transfer pan from oven to a heat-safe surface, such as a cold burner on your stovetop. Set aside for 5 minutes.

Step 6:

Sprinkle flour on a flat, clean, dry work surface.

Step 7:

Transfer the dough from the bowl to the work surface. Using a knife or dough blade, cut the dough into 8 equal-sized pieces.

Step 8:

Using your hands, shape dough into a 1/2" circle of even thickness.

Step 9:

On the floured work surface, using a rolling pin, press down and roll out from the center of the dough ball, over and over, each time rolling in a different direction, until you roll out a 6" circle of even thickness. Set aside.

Step 10:

Repeat Steps 8 & 9 for all remaining dough pieces.

Step 11:

In a pan, medium-high heat, add just enough peanut oil to cover the bottom of the pan. If during the frying process the oil begins to give off smoke, then turn down the heat.

Step 12:

Place 1 circle of dough gently into the oil. Avoid splashing the oil. If more than 1 will fit side by side with another in the same pan, then add another.

Step 13:

Fry 1 minute, until light golden-brown colored on the bottom side.

Step 14:

With a spatula or turner, gently flip the pancake over, then fry for another 1 minute, until light golden-brown on the bottom side.

Step 15:

Transfer fried pancake to a plate. Set aside.

Step 16:
Repeat Steps 12 - 15 for all remaining pancakes, stacking the completed pancakes on top of each other.

Step 17:
With a sharp knife, cut thin slices of duck breasts,

Step 18:
Retrieve a pancake, then place a portion of duck slices into center of pancake, then roll or fold up. Set aside.

Step 19:
Repeat Step 18 for all remaining duck slices and pancakes.

Step 20:
Additional Hoisin can be used for dipping sauce.

Fresh Storage:

For any duck slices and pancakes not assembled, place in separate containers, cover with plastic wrap / film or place in separate plastic sealable bags and store in the refrigerator. Reheat in a pan. Use within 2 days.

Frozen Storage:

For any duck and pancakes NOT assembled, place in separate containers, cover with plastic wrap / film or place in separate plastic sealable bags and store in the freezer. Remove from freezer and transfer to refrigerator to thaw before use. Reheat in a pan. May be frozen up to 1 week.

Your Notes:

_____

MOVIE FOUR

Course #3: Almond Float with Cherries

Ingredients:

1/2 cup warm water (80 – 100 degrees)

2 & 1/2 oz packet of unflavored gelatin

1/2 cup cold tap water

2 cups whole (3%) dairy milk

1/2 cup sugar

2 tsp almond extract

1 cup whole fresh sweet cherries, pitted

Directions:

Step 1:

In a bowl, add warm water and gelatin, then stir or whisk to dissolve gelatin. Set aside.

Step 2:

In a pot, high heat, add water, then bring to boil.

Step 3:

Add gelatin mixture, then stir well.

Step 4:

Add milk, sugar, and extract, then stir, until dissolves.

Step 5:

Pour the mix in equal amounts into 4 clear, colorless, glass dessert-sized bowls, goblets, martini glasses, or parfait glasses.

Step 6:

Cover with plastic wrap / film. Transfer to refrigerator to chill, at least 4 hours, until it looks like a pudding.

Step 7:

Add 1/4 cup cherries, to top of each almond float.

Fresh Storage:

Cover bowls with plastic wrap / film and store in the refrigerator. Use within 3 days.

Frozen Storage:
Do NOT freeze.

Round One Guess As to the Inspirational Movie:

MOVIE FOUR

Level One Hint:

- The inspired dish was served during the first Sunday dinner and during the cooking preparation the main ingredient is inflated.

Round Two Guess As to the Inspirational Movie:

MOVIE FOUR

Level Two Hints:

- At an important banquet, the shark fin soup is found to be bad and in need of replacement.
- The protagonist's youngest daughter works at Wendy's.
- The protagonist is a Chef who is so concerned with the freshness of food as to raise his own chickens and to keep live fish in a clay pot in the kitchen.
- In the opening cooking sequence, an impressive, 3-tier collection of knives is shown in the protagonist's home kitchen.

Round Three Guess As to the Inspirational Movie:

MOVIE FOUR

Level Three Hints:

- Peking Duck Pancakes
- Chu has a secret romance with Jin-Rong during the inspirational film.
- Tai Pei is the setting for the inspirational film, although Chu's middle daughter almost moves to Amsterdam.
- The originally delivered script was based upon research on Chinese culture and was rejected by the director; the accepted revision was considered as depicting Chinese culture even though it was based upon a stereotypical Jewish family with Chinese names, setting, and food.

Round Four Guess As to the Inspirational Movie:

MOVIE FIVE

Course #1: Broccoli Salad

Ingredients:

1/4 cup pecans, whole or pieces

1 tsp sugar

1 Tbsp white vinegar

zest of 1 lemon

1 Tbsp lemon juice

2 tsp mustard (the condiment)

1 tsp salt

1/4 cup extra virgin olive oil

1/2 cup grape tomatoes, cut in half

4 cups broccoli, cut off and discard thick stems, then cut
    bushy "florets" into chunks, no thicker than 1/4"

2 Tbsp basil, stemmed and chopped – chop 1 full
    pass through herbs to keep from bruising leaves

Directions:

Step 1:

In a pan, medium heat, add pecans, then toast about 5 minutes, turning over frequently with spoon / spatula, until fragrant. Be careful not to burn these.

Step 2:

Transfer pan to a heat-safe surface, such as a cold stovetop burner, then set aside to cool.

Step 3:

In a bowl, add sugar, vinegar, zest, lemon juice, mustard, and salt, then whisk well. While whisking vigorously and continuously, slowly drizzle in oil to form an emulsion.

Step 4:

Add grape tomatoes, broccoli, and basil, then use a spoon / spatula to toss contents to coat evenly with emulsion.

Step 5:

Cover with plastic wrap / film. Transfer to refrigerator for at least 1 hour. Use by the next day.

Step 6:
Just before serving, add pecans.

Fresh Storage:
Cover with plastic wrap / film or place in a plastic sealable bag and store in the refrigerator. Use within 3 days.

Frozen Storage:
Do NOT freeze.

Your Notes:

_____

_____

MOVIE FIVE

Course #2: Chicken Marsala

Bread: Frequently Used Side Item Recipes

Ingredients:

4 6 oz boneless skinless chicken breasts

1/2 cup flour

1 tsp salt

1/4 tsp ground black pepper

1 Tbsp butter

1 Tbsp olive oil

2 cups white button mushrooms, sliced

1 cup chicken stock / broth

1/2 cup Marsala cooking wine (store: near vinegars, oils)

1 cup heavy cream

additional salt and pepper, to taste

rolling pin or meat tenderizer mallet

Directions:

Step 1:

Preheat oven to 350 degrees.

Step 2:

In a bowl, add flour, salt, and pepper, then stir to mix well.

Step 3:

Place chicken between 2 pieces of plastic wrap / film.
Using rolling pin or flat side of meat tenderizer mallet,
pound the chicken until uniformly 1/4" thick. Set aside.

Step 4:

To the flour mixture bowl, add chicken pieces, dragging
back and forth through mixture until chicken pieces are
coated well on all sides. Set aside.

Step 5:

In oven-safe pan, medium heat, add butter and oil, then
stir to mix. Cook until butter melted.

Step 6:

Add chicken pieces, then cook until bottom side is
brown colored. Flip chicken pieces with spatula / tongs,
then cook until bottom side is brown colored.

Step 7:

Add mushrooms, stock, and wine, then cook, stirring occasionally, until mushrooms get softer and shrink.

Step 8:

Transfer pan into preheated oven, on the middle rack. Bake for 30 minutes, until sauce begins to thicken.

Step 9:

In last few minutes of marsala baking time, cut bread into slices thick enough for dipping. Set aside.

Step 10:

Add cream, then stir well. Add salt and pepper, to taste.

Step 11:

Either serve bread on a plate alongside bowls of chicken marsala OR line empty bowl with bread so that edges stand above rim of bowl then add chicken marsala to middle of bowl.

Fresh Storage:

Cover chicken marsala (separately from the bread) with plastic wrap / film or place in a plastic sealable container and store in the refrigerator. Reheat in a pan. Use within 5 days.

Either wrap bread and store on countertop OR store in a bread box. Use within 2 days.

Frozen Storage:

Cover chicken marsala (separately from the bread) with plastic wrap / film or place in a plastic sealable container, and store in freezer. Remove from freezer, then reheat in a pan on low heat. May be frozen up to 1 month.

Do NOT freeze the bread.

Your Notes:

_____

_____

MOVIE FIVE

Course #3: English Trifle

(Time Management: angel food cake and lemon custard can be prepared 1 day in advance and stored separately. 4 total elements to be prepared/needed before assembling trifle: angel food cake, lemon custard, Chambord cream, and fresh fruit)

Angel Food Cake Ingredients:
1 & 1/2 cups powdered sugar
1 cup cake flour
1 & 1/2 cups egg whites
1 & 1/2 tsp "cream of tartar" (in grocery with spices)
1 cup sugar
1 & 1/2 tsp vanilla extract
1/2 tsp almond extract
1/4 tsp salt
angel food cake pan or Bundt cake pan, lightly sprayed
    with non-stick cooking oil spray

Angel Food Cake Directions:

Step 1:

Preheat oven to 375 degrees.

Step 2:

In a bowl, add powdered sugar and flour, then whisk to mix well.

Step 3:

In a mixing bowl, with a hand or stand mixer, add egg whites and cream of tartar, then beat, on medium speed, until foamy.

Step 4:

Increase mixer to high speed, slowly add sugar (about 1/4 cup at a time).

Step 5:

Add vanilla extract, almond extract, and salt, then beat until mixture reaches "stiff peaks". Remove beaters from bowl.

Checking for peaks:
Soft peaks are formed when you quickly dip the mixing beaters in and out once, pulling up some of the mixture into a peak but having it fall back down immediately into the rest of the mixture. Stiff peaks are formed the same way but stay in the peak shape and do not fall down – like the topping of a meringue pie.

Step 6:
Gently sprinkle in about 1/3 of flour & sugar mix, then using a spatula, gently fold in. Repeat the adding of the mixture and folding in, until all batter is mixed.

Step 7:
Transfer batter into prepared cake pan. Place the pan into the preheated oven, on the middle rack. Bake for 30 minutes, until top of cake is spongy, springs back when touched, and is just lightly golden-brown colored.

Step 8:
Remove pan from oven, turn pan upside down on a wire rack, and set aside to cool for 2 hours.

Step 9:

Turn the pan upright. Using a long knife or thin spatula, run the knife along the inner edge of the pan until the entire cake has been loosened from the pan. Remove the pan.

Angel Food Cake Fresh Storage:

If assembling trifle soon, then set angel food cake aside. OR If assembling trifle the next day, then wrap angel food cake in plastic wrap / film and either store in the refrigerator or on the countertop. Use in 1 day.

Angel Food Cake Frozen Storage:

Do not freeze.

Your Notes:

_____

_____

Lemon Custard Ingredients:

5 eggs - separated and yolks only kept

1 cup sugar

1 Tbsp cornstarch

1 & 1/2 cups whole (3%) diary milk

1/2 cup lemon juice

Custard Equipment:

2 mixing size bowls - one needs to fit inside the other

1 separate mixing bowl for the egg mixture - any size that fits the ingredients

fine-mesh strainer - any size, as just pouring liquid through it

enough ice cubes to fill the larger bowl half-way

heat-safe whisk

heat-safe spatula

candy-style thermometer

Custard Notes:

Get out all of the equipment you will need and measure your ingredients ahead of time and have ready to use, as if you were going to make a television cooking show. Time and temperature are important when making custard, so you do not want to pause between steps to fetch and/or measure anything.

Lemon Custard Directions:

Step 1:

In the larger mixing bowl, add ice cubes until the bowl is half-full. This will be used to make an "ice bath" later. Set aside.

Step 2:

On the smaller mixing bowl, place the fine-mesh strainer. Set aside.

Step 3:

In a pan, on medium heat, add milk and bring to simmer (almost boiling but not at full boil).

Step 4: Transfer to a heat-safe surface, such as a cold burner on your stovetop. Add lemon juice. Set aside.

Step 5:

In any mixing bowl, add egg yolks, sugar, and cornstarch, then whisk to mix well. *Do not allow sugar and egg to sit or the eggs will chemically cook and ruin the consistency of your custard; immediately move on to the next step.

Step 6:

In a slow and steady stream, drizzle warm milk mixture, whisking vigorously the entire time. *Adding the milk mix too quickly will scramble the eggs. Set the empty pan aside.

Step 7:

Transfer custard mixture from the bowl back into the same pan as used before. Place the candy-style thermometer into the pan, the tip of the candy thermometer should not touch the bottom of the pan.

Step 8:

On low heat, with a spatula, continuously stir custard mixture, until the mixture thickens and reaches 170 degrees.

Step 9:

Transfer the custard mixture to the clean, smaller bowl, using the fine-mesh strainer on top of it to strain out solid pieces from the custard mixture.

Step 10:

Transfer the smaller bowl into the larger bowl with the "ice bath", then with a spatula, continuously stir custard mixture, until custard mixture reaches temperature of 40 degrees.

Custard Fresh Storage:

Immediately cover in plastic wrap / film and store in the refrigerator. Use in 1 day.

Custard Frozen Storage:

Do not freeze.

Your Notes:

_____

_____

Chambord Cream Ingredients:

1 & 1/4 oz packet of unflavored gelatin

1/8 cup warm water (80 – 100 degrees)

2 cups heavy cream

4 Tbsp Chambord liqueur

1/4 cup sugar

Chambord Cream Directions:

Step 1:

In a bowl, add warm water and gelatin, then stir or whisk to dissolve gelatin. Set aside.

Step 2:

In a mixing bowl, with a hand or stand mixer, add cream, then beat on high speed.

Step 3:

Continuing on high speed, add sugar and Chambord.

Step 4:

Continuing on high speed, add gelatin mixture, then beat to stiff peaks.

Checking for stiff peaks:
Stiff peaks are formed when you quickly dip the mixing beaters in and out once, pulling up some of the mixture into a peak, then it stays in the peak shape and does not fall down – like the topping of a meringue pie.

Step 5:
Cover bowl with plastic wrap / film. Set aside in refrigerator, until ready to assemble trifle.

Your Notes:

_____

_____

Fresh Fruit Ingredients:
1 cup fresh raspberries
1 cup fresh strawberries, cored and quartered
1 cup fresh blackberries

Fresh Fruit Directions:
In a bowl, add berries, then gently stir to mix well. Set aside.

Trifle Assembly!!!:

Trifle is usually assembled into a large, clear, colorless, glass bowl, commonly with uniform sides and a built-in pedestal base. As a substitute, you can build each person an individual-sized trifle in a clear, colorless, glass dessert-sized bowl, goblet, martini glass, or parfait glass. you want to be able to enjoy the view of the layering of the ingredients with their vibrant colors and varying textures.

All 4 elements should be layered to make a complete layer, and you should make 3 complete layers in the bowl.

Trifle Directions:

Step 1:

Transfer the angel food cake to the work surface. Tear or cut the angel food cake into 1" x 1" pieces. Add pieces to a bowl.

Step 2:

Retrieve other 3 elements and place on a work surface.

Step 3:

Set up with 4 separate utensils for building the trifle. Set out the trifle bowl (or substitutes).

Step 4:
In a trifle bowl, add a layer of angel food cake pieces, using 1/3 of the total pieces, to make 1 jumbled-uneven layer.

Step 5:
Add a layer of custard, using 1/3 of the total custard.

Step 6:
Add a layer of fresh fruit, using 1/3 of the total berries.

Step 7:
Add a layer of Chambord cream, using 1/3 of the total cream.

Step 8:
Repeat Steps 4 - 7 for 2 more complete layers of the 4 elements.

Step 9:
Cover bowl with plastic wrap / film and refrigerate at least 1 hour before serving.

Trifle Fresh Storage:

Cover with plastic wrap / film and store in the refrigerator. Use within 2 days.

Trifle Frozen Storage:

Do NOT freeze trifle. Ever. It's likely a crime – you don't want to know.

Your Notes:

_____

_____

Round One Guess As to the Inspirational Movie:

_____

MOVIE FIVE

Level One Hint:

- The inspired dish is a sign of change in the inspirational movie, is the protagonist's daughter's favorite dish which she is rationed to only one a day, and is what the daughter gets the patrons to try so that they become regular diners.

Round Two Guess As to the Inspirational Movie:

_____

MOVIE FIVE

Level Two Hints:

- One of the top food critics in the inspirational movie has a television show called Food for Thought, which has a segment that is a guide to Chefs who he thinks have talent and originality, although he is a handful for his staff due to being an alcoholic.
- The restaurant that the protagonist had with his wife was called World's End, and the one that he opens with his reassembled kitchen team is called The Boot.
- The protagonist throws a microwave out the front door of The Boot.

Round Three Guess As to the Inspirational Movie:

_____

MOVIE FIVE

Level Three Hints:

- English Trifle
- The Boot has a sign up warding off dogs and critics, although two food critics appear in the cast and make a big difference personally and professionally to the protagonist, including one of them having an "ex" who brings him a rat problem.
- The protagonist has a shrine set up with the cell phone his wife was talking on when she died in a car accident, a picture of his wife, and the urn with her ashes.
- The protagonist is friends with Gordon Ramsey, who plays himself in the cast.

Round Four Guess As to the Inspirational Movie:

_____

MOVIE SIX

Course #1: Couscous Salad

Ingredients:

1 cup chicken stock / broth

3/4 cup couscous

1 cup roma tomatoes, diced

1 cup cucumber, peeled and diced

1/2 cup kalamata olives, pitted and cut in half

3 green onions, sliced thinly

1 Tbsp dried dill weed

2 Tbsp lemon juice

zest of one lemon

2 Tbsp extra virgin olive oil

1/8 tsp salt

3 Tbsp Greek feta cheese

Directions:

Step 1:

In a pot, medium heat, add stock, then bring to boil.

Step 2:

Add couscous, then cover pot with lid and transfer to a heat-safe surface such as a cold stovetop burner. Set aside 5 minutes.

Step 3:

Remove lid, then transfer warm couscous to a bowl. Set aside to cool.

Step 4:

Add tomatoes, cucumber, olives, onions, and dried dill, then stir to mix. Set aside.

Step 5:

In another bowl, add lemon juice, zest, salt and oil, then whisk to mix well. Pour this over couscous, then stir to mix well.

Step 6:
Cover couscous salad with plastic wrap / film, then transfer to refrigerator, set aside at least 1 hour before serving. Use within 1 day.

Step 7:
Just before serving, sprinkle with feta cheese.

Fresh Storage:
Cover with plastic wrap / film and store in the refrigerator. Use within 7 days.

Frozen Storage:
Do NOT freeze.

Your Notes:

_____

_____

MOVIE SIX

Course #2: Greek Meatballs served with Sauce and Vermicelli

Vermicelli:

8 oz Vermicelli pasta cooked according to package

Greek Meatballs Ingredients:

1 cup breadcrumbs (Panko)

1/4 cup whole (3%) dairy milk

1/2 lb ground lamb

1/2 lb ground beef

2 eggs, beaten

2 Tbsp red onion, minced

1 Tbsp fresh oregano, chopped finely

1 Tbsp fresh mint, chopped finely

1 Tbsp garlic, minced

1 tsp ground cinnamon

1 tsp salt

1/2 tsp ground black pepper

1/2 tsp paprika

1/4 tsp allspice

2 Tbsp vegetable oil

Greek Meatballs Directions:

Step 1:

In a bowl, add breadcrumbs and milk, then set aside to soak for 5 minutes.

Step 2:

Add lamb, beef, eggs, onion, oregano, mint, garlic, cinnamon, salt, pepper, paprika, and allspice, then using bare hands, mix well.

Step 3:

Using your bare hands, take a portion of the mixture and roll it around in circles in your hands to shape a meatball about the size of a golf ball. Set aside on a plate.

Step 4:

Repeat Step 3 until all mixture has been made into meatballs.

Step 5:
In a pan, medium-high heat, add oil and meatballs, then cook meatballs, turning and moving around every few minutes, to brown evenly.

Step 6:
Transfer meatballs to a clean bowl, then set aside.

Sauce Ingredients:
2 Tbsp olive oil
1/2 cup red onion, diced
28 oz canned pre-diced plain tomatoes (do not drain)
1 Tbsp fresh oregano, chopped
1 Tbsp fresh mint, chopped
1 bay leaf
1/2 cinnamon stick
1/2 tsp allspice
salt, to taste
4 oz Greek feta cheese

Sauce Directions:
Step 1:
In a pan, medium heat, add oil and onion, then cook for 3 minutes.

Step 2:

Add tomatoes with juice, oregano, mint, bay leaf, cinnamon stick, and allspice, then stir to mix.

Step 3:

Add browned meatballs, then cook for 20 minutes.

Step 4:

Remove bay leaf and cinnamon stick. Add salt, to taste.

Step 5:

Spoon meatballs and sauce over vermicelli, then sprinkle feta crumbles over top.

Fresh Storage:

Cover with plastic wrap / film and store in the refrigerator. Reheat in a pan. Use within 3 days.

Frozen Storage:

Do NOT freeze.

Your Notes:

_____

_____

MOVIE SIX

Course #3: Plum & Almond Crumble

Ingredients:

1 cup butter

1 cup sugar

3 cups ground almonds (or ground from whole/slivered
in coffee/spice grinder or food processor)

1 cup flour

2 Tbsp flour

2 eggs, beaten

1 tsp cinnamon

1 tsp baking powder

6 plums, stoned and cut into 6 equal pieces each
(if you cannot find plums, then pears are an
excellent substitute, using 4 pears, cored and cut)

1 Tbsp sugar

1/2 cup slivered almonds

Directions:

Step 1:

Preheat oven to 350 degrees.

Step 2:

Lightly coat a 9 x 13" pan with nonstick cooking oil spray. Set aside.

Step 3:

In a bowl, add butter, sugar, and ground almonds, then mix well, until mealy.

Step 4:

Transfer half of the mix to another bowl, and set aside.

Step 5:

Add 1 cup flour to the remaining half, then mix well.

Step 6:

Transfer to the prepared pan, then spread evenly across entire bottom of pan.

Step 7:

Place pan into preheated oven, on the middle rack. Bake 15 minutes, until golden-brown colored.

Step 8:
Remove pan from the oven and place on a heat-safe surface, such as a cold stovetop. Set aside 15 minutes to cool.

Step 9:
In set-aside-half mix, add 2 Tbsp flour, cinnamon, eggs, and baking powder, then mix well.

Step 10:
Transfer 4 Tbsp of mix to another bowl, set aside.

Step 11:
Spread the remaining mixture into the prepared pan.

Step 12:
Add plum pieces evenly.

Step 13:
Sprinkle 1 Tbsp of sugar evenly over all.

Step 14:
Sprinkle slivered almonds evenly over all.

Step 15:
Sprinkle set-aside-mix evenly over all.

Step 16:
Place pan into preheated oven, on the middle rack. Bake for 20 minutes, until golden colored.

Step 17:
Remove pan and place on a heat-safe surface, such as a cold stovetop. Cool slightly before serving.

Fresh Storage:
Cover with plastic wrap / film and store in the refrigerator. Use within 7 days.

Frozen Storage:
Do NOT freeze.

Your Notes:

Round One Guess As to the Inspirational Movie:

MOVIE SIX

Level One Hint:

- The inspired dish is an alteration, made by the protagonist, to his mother's cooking, when he tries to stop his parents from arguing; the recipe change only makes another argument possible.

Round Two Guess As to the Inspirational Movie:

MOVIE SIX

Level Two Hints:

- In this inspirational movie, mussels are equated with women in love and with men having discussions in a hammam (Turkish bath).

- The movie is broken down into 3 parts, all associating with 3 courses in a meal: appetizer, main course (entrée), and dessert. Appetizers are discussed as means to foretell you of what types of flavors are coming next in the meal sequence, similar to how the first portion of a movie foretells the course that the movie is likely to take.

- The protagonist learns how to interpret wars, cuisine, and behaviors by the spices used.

- The wrong spice can be used to say something, such as when using cumin versus cinnamon.

Round Three Guess As to the Inspirational Movie:

MOVIE SIX

Level Three Hints:

- Greek Meatballs served with Sauce and Vermicelli

- The protagonist is an astronomer and a professor; he first learned about astronomy through spices lessons from his grandfather, a spice shop owner in Istanbul in 1959.

- When the protagonist's family is deported from Turkey to their native Greece, Saime gives Fanis a toy kitchen.

- In Athens, the priests pray and the parents plot against the protagonist cooking.

- Fanis returns to the ruins of his grandfather's spice shop, finds remnants of old spices, breathes on the combination, and has a vision of planets all around him.

Round Four Guess As to the Inspirational Movie:

MOVIE SEVEN

Course #1: Red & White Bites

Ingredients:
16 Peppadew cherry peppers
4 oz herbed garlic goat cheese (Boursin or any other)
3 Tbsp crème fraîche

Directions:
Step 1:
Drain Peppadew cherry peppers. Remove tops (if present), then set aside.

Step 2:
In a bowl, add goat cheese and crème fraîche, then vigorously whisk, until light and fluffy.

Step 3:
Spoon a portion of cheese mixture into each of the cherry peppers. Cover with plastic wrap / film, then transfer to the refrigerator for 30 minutes to chill.

Fresh Storage:

Cover with plastic wrap / film or place in a plastic sealable bag and store in the refrigerator. Use within 1 day.

Frozen Storage:

Do NOT freeze.

Your Notes:

_____

_____

MOVIE SEVEN

Course #2: Black & Blue Mussels served with Herbed Gnocchi ("no-key")

Herbed Gnocchi Ingredients:

3/4 cup water

6 Tbsp butter

2 tsp salt

1 cup flour

1 Tbsp Dijon mustard

1 tsp fresh parsley, chopped finely

1 tsp fresh thyme, chopped finely

1 tsp fresh basil, chopped finely

Herbed Gnocchi Directions:

Step 1:

In a pot, medium heat, add water, butter, and salt, then mix well.

Step 2:

Increase heat to high, then bring to simmer (almost boiling but not at full boil).

Step 3:

Reduce heat to medium and add flour, then stir continuously with a spoon / spatula, until the dough mix pulls away from the bottom and sides of the pan. The dough should look glossy.

Step 4:

Continue to cook dough for another 5 minutes, stirring constantly, while the dough will steam and you will smell the flour.

Step 5:

Transfer the dough to a mixing bowl with a hand or stand mixer, medium speed.

Step 6:

Add mustard and herbs, then mix well.

Step 7:

Continuing medium speed, add the eggs, one at a time, then mix well. Add the next egg only when the previous egg is fully incorporated. Set aside for 30 minutes, to cool.

Step 8:
Cover a plate with a few layers of paper towels. Set
aside.

Step 9:
In a pot, medium-high heat, add at least 3 quarts of
water. Add enough salt so that the water is noticeably
salty.

Step 10:
Increase to high heat, bring to simmer (almost boiling but
not at full boil), and adjust temp to maintain simmer.
Keep simmering while complete next several steps.

Step 11:
Using a table-teaspoon in each hand, scoop out 1 tsp
of dough. Hold the spoons facing each other and twist
in opposing directions to form dough into the shape of
an American football. Gently drop the gnocchi piece
into the simmering water.

Step 12:

Repeat Step 11 until all of the gnocchi is in the water. Keep an eye on the pieces in the water while making more pieces to put in to the water.

Step 13:

Once a gnocchi piece floats, then continue to cook it for 1 minute. With a slotted spoon, remove the gnocchi piece as soon as it is done cooking, and transfer it to the prepared plate. Set aside to dry.

Step 14:

Repeat Step 13 until all of the gnocchi are cooked and drying. Set aside.

Fresh Storage:

Cover gnocchi that has not been used in a dish with plastic wrap / film and store in the refrigerator. Reheat in a pan, on medium-low heat. Use within 2 days.

Frozen Storage:

Cover gnocchi that has not been used in a dish with plastic wrap / film, and store in freezer. Remove from freezer and place on countertop to thaw before use. Reheat in a pan, on medium-low heat. May be frozen up to 4 weeks.

Your Notes:

_____

_____

Black & Blue Mussels Ingredients:

3 lbs fresh mussels

1/3 cup applewood smoked bacon, diced

4 Tbsp olive oil

1/3 cup shallots, sliced thinly

1/2 cup Chardonnay wine (more dry)

1/2 cup Bleu Cheese

1/2 cup chicken stock / broth

juice of 1 lemon

Attention: Make sure the mussels are fresh and alive before use! If these are cracked or do not close up when tapped on, then do not use. If you are uncomfortable with purchasing mussels alone, then seek out a fresh seafood purveyor to ask for guidance. Do NOT eat questionable seafood! Spoiled seafood can cause serious health issues, including death.

Black & Blue Mussels Directions:
Step 1:
Rinse mussels in cool water, checking again to make sure that these are all healthy. Discard any mussels that do not close up.

Step 2:
In a pot, medium-high heat, add diced bacon, then cook and flip when bottom side is starting to brown, until bacon pieces are done but still soft.

Step 3:
Add, oil, shallots, and cooked & dry gnocchi, then stir and cook, until gnocchi starts to turn golden-brown color on bottom side.

Step 4:
Flip gnocchi, then cook, until starts to turn golden-brown color on bottom side.

Step 5:
Add mussels and wine. Cover the pot with a tight-fitting lid, then cook for 3-5 minutes, until mussels open up.

Step 6:
Add chicken stock, bleu cheese, and lemon juice. Cover again, then cook for 2 minutes.

Step 7:
Stir, check broth, then add salt and pepper, to taste.

Fresh/Frozen Storage:

Do NOT store.

Your Notes:

_____

MOVIE SEVEN

Course #3: Gold & Amber Bread Pudding served with Pecan Sauce

Gold & Amber Bread Pudding Ingredients:

1 loaf of day-old bread (baguette, Challah, cinnamon
swirl, etc...)

1/3 cup golden raisins

1/2 cups sugar

3 cups dairy heavy whipping cream

2 Tbsp vanilla extract

5 eggs, beaten

1 tsp cinnamon

8x8" baking pan and another pan with sides which are at
least 2" tall that the 8x8" pan will fit into

Gold & Amber Bread Pudding Directions:

Step 1:

Preheat oven to 325 degrees.

Step 2:

Lightly coat the inside of an 8x8" baking pan (bottom
and sides) with nonstick cooking oil spray. Set aside.

Step 3:

Tear or cut the bread into 1" cube pieces and toss into the prepared pan. Fill the baking pan to the rim with bread pieces.

Step 4:

Evenly sprinkle raisins over bread, then using hands, mix until raisins are evenly distributed. Set aside.

Step 5:

In a bowl, add sugar, cream, vanilla extract, eggs, and cinnamon, then whisk to mix well.

Step 6:

Pour liquid over the bread pieces. Push down on bread pieces to soak all well.

Step 7:

Place the 8 x 8 pan into the larger pan and put in enough hot tap water to come up 1" on the sides of the pan (this double-pan method creates a "water bath" to give even cooking throughout).

Step 8:

Place the double-pan set into the preheated oven, on the middle rack. Bake for 45 minutes.

Step 9:

Check at the center of the bread pudding, with a toothpick inserted straight down and for approximately 3/4 the length of the toothpick, then wiggle the toothpick a bit to make a hole large enough to not scrape the edges of the toothpick as it is removed. If done, then the toothpick should be "clean" or dry after removed, without wet batter sticking to it. (If not "clean", then bake a few minutes more and recheck. Repeat until "clean".)

Step 10:

Remove double-pan set from oven and place on a heat-safe surface, such as a cold stovetop. Carefully remove the inner pan from its "water bath" and place it on a wire rack that has a dish-towel covering it. Set aside.

Pecan Sauce Ingredients:

1 stick butter, softened from having sat on a countertop
at room temperature

1 cup dark brown sugar

3 Tbsp whole (3%) dairy milk

1 tsp vanilla extract

1/4 cup chopped pecans

Pecan Sauce Directions:

Step 1:

In a pot, medium heat, add butter and sugar, then stir occasionally, until mix comes to boil.

Step 2:

Remove from heat and place on a heat-safe surface, such as a cold stovetop burner.

Step 3:

Add milk, vanilla extract, and pecans, then stir to mix well. Set aside for 3 minutes.

Step 4:

Pour warm sauce over warm bread pudding, then serve warm.

Fresh Storage:

Cover with plastic wrap / film or place in a plastic sealable bag and store in the refrigerator. Serve chilled OR reheat in the baking pan, in the oven, at 350 degrees, covered with aluminum foil, for 15 minutes. Use within 5 days.

Frozen Storage:

Cover dish with plastic wrap / film or place in a plastic sealable bag, and store in freezer. Remove from freezer and transfer to refrigerator to thaw before use. Serve chilled OR reheat in the baking pan, in the oven, at 350 degrees, covered with aluminum foil, for 15 minutes. May be frozen up to 2 weeks.

Your Notes:

_____

_____

Round One Guess As to the Inspirational Movie:

_____

MOVIE SEVEN

Level One Hint:

- The inspired dish is named after the two bookie baddies in the inspirational film.

Round Two Guess As to the Inspirational Movie:

MOVIE SEVEN

Level Two Hints:

- The male protagonist is a star Chef named Udo, who teaches 3 proper responses to a Chef.
- Nino is "86'd" (fired) due to working with a dull knife in the kitchen.
- Udo's father is the owner of the restaurant and wants traditional food, but Udo has much to say in reaction to this.
- Like many NYC restaurants, the kitchen is in the basement of the restaurant, the seating is crowded in the dining room, and the surprise visit of a famous food critic makes the Chef a busy man.

Round Three Guess As to the Inspirational Movie:

_____

MOVIE SEVEN

Level Three Hints:

- Black and Blue Mussels served with Herbed Gnocchi
- Duncan is the Sous Chef with a gambling problem who owes $6500 to Black and Blue, but his debt is paid by Udo's father, Julio (aka Lewis, aka GG) to save his life.
- A $5 bet will get you an answer from the bartender with encyclopedic trivia knowledge.
- Tribeca in NYC is home to a film festival and is the setting for this inspirational, independent feature movie from 2000.
- Electricity service stops in the middle of dinner service, so candles and flashlights are employed to keep this trendy restaurant in full swing.

Round Four Guess As to the Inspirational Movie:

MOVIE EIGHT

Course #1: Italian Salad served with Italian Dressing

Italian Dressing Ingredients:
2 Tbsp white wine vinegar
1 Tbsp lemon juice
6 Tbsp extra virgin olive oil
2 Tbsp fresh parsley, chopped
1/2 tsp salt
2 garlic cloves, peeled, smashed, and chopped
1 tsp dried basil
1/4 tsp red pepper flakes
1/2 tsp dried oregano

Italian Dressing Directions:
Step 1:
In a bowl, add vinegar and lemon juice, then whisk to mix.

Step 2:
While whisking vigorously and continuously, slowly drizzle in oil to form an emulsion.

Step 3:
Add parsley, salt, garlic, basil, red pepper flakes, oregano, then whisk to mix well. Set aside.

Fresh Storage:
Cover Italian Dressing with plastic wrap / film or place in a plastic sealable bag or place in a glass bottle with a stopper or a pourer and store in the refrigerator. Use within 3 days.

Frozen Storage:
Do NOT freeze.

Your Notes:

_____

_____

Salad Ingredients:

4 cups romaine (or baby romaine), chopped
8 grape tomatoes, cut in half

1 cucumber, peeled, seeded, and diced (cut in half from end to end, then use a spoon to scoop out the seeded middle, like carving out a canoe boat)

1/4 red onion, sliced thinly

8 pepperoncini

1/4 cup carrot, grated

Salad Directions:

Step 1:

In a bowl, add all salad ingredients, then using bare hands or large spoons, toss to mix well.

Step 2:

Drizzle Italian Dressing over salad, then toss to mix well.

Fresh/Frozen Storage:

Do NOT store.

Your Notes:

_____

_____

MOVIE EIGHT

Course #2: Spaghetti & Meatballs served with Marinara Sauce & with Garlic Bread

Baguette Bread: Frequently Used Side Item Recipes

Garlic Bread Ingredients:

Baguette Bread

1 cup butter, softened from having sat on a countertop
at room temperature

1/3 cup olive oil

2 Tbsp garlic, peeled, smashed, and minced

2 tsp garlic salt

Directions:

Step 1:

When baguettes have been placed on a wire rack to cool, decrease oven to 450 degrees. Set aside baguettes for 5 minutes, to cool.

Step 2:
If broiler is inside of main oven space, then make sure that 1 oven rack is in the middle position and that another oven rack is in the top position.

Step 3:
With a serrated/bread knife, cut a baguette in half from the side, to create a top and a bottom half that will each lay flat.

Step 4:
Repeat Step 2 for all remaining baguette loaves. Set aside.

Step 5:
In a pot, low heat, add butter, oil, garlic, and garlic salt, then stir to mix well. Cook, stirring frequently, until butter is melted.

Step 6:
Remove from heat and place on a heat-safe surface, such as a cold stovetop burner.

Step 7:

Using a pastry brush, generously coat the crumb-side of the cut baguette half with warm garlic butter mix. Transfer coated half to a baking sheet. Set aside.

Step 8:

Repeat Step 7 for all remaining baguette halves.

Step 9:

Place sheet(s) into the preheated oven, on the middle rack. Bake for 5 minutes.

Step 10:

Turn oven heat off. Turn broil (low) on.

Step 11:

If broiler is inside the main oven space, then transfer baking sheet to top oven rack position OR If broiler is in a separate area, then transfer baking rack to that broiler space.

Step 12:

Broil bread to toast it, 3-5 minutes, until top of bread is lightly browned.

Fresh Storage:

Cover baked garlic bread with plastic wrap / film or place in a plastic sealable bag and store in the refrigerator. Reheat in the oven, at 350 degrees, on a baking sheet, for 5 minutes. Use within 5 days.

Frozen Storage:

Cover baked garlic bread with plastic wrap / film or place in a plastic sealable bag, and store in freezer. Remove from freezer. Reheat in the oven, at 350 degrees, on a baking sheet, for 5 minutes. May be frozen up to 3 weeks.

Your Notes:

_____

_____

Spaghetti:

Cook 4 servings of spaghetti noodles according to package directions.

Meatballs Ingredients:

1/2 lb ground hamburger (any fat ratio that you prefer)

1/2 lb ground veal (at grocery, ask at your meat/deli
counter if this is not in the regular meat section)

10 oz mild Italian sausage, cut or broken into small pieces

1/2 cup breadcrumbs (Panko)

1/2 cup Parmesan cheese, shredded

1/2 cup yellow onion, diced

1 tsp garlic, peeled, smashed, and minced

1 tsp dried oregano

1 tsp salt

1 egg, beaten

Meatballs Directions:

Step 1:

In a bowl, add ground hamburger, ground veal, sausage, breadcrumbs, Parmesan cheese, onion, garlic, oregano, salt, and egg, then using bare hands, mix well.

Step 2:

Using your bare hands, take a portion of the mixture and roll it around in circles in your hands to shape a meatball about the size of a golf ball. Set aside on a plate.

Step 3:
Repeat Step 2 until all mixture has been made into meatballs.

Step 4:
In a pan, medium-high heat, add meatballs, then cook meatballs, turning and moving around every few minutes, to brown evenly.

Step 5:
Transfer meatballs to a clean bowl, then set aside.

Marinara Sauce Ingredients:
2 tsp olive oil
1/2 yellow onion, diced
1 tsp garlic, peeled, smashed, and minced
16 oz canned diced tomatoes
16 oz can plain tomato sauce
1 bay leaf
1 tsp oregano
1/2 tsp basil
salt, to taste
ground black pepper, to taste

Marinara Sauce Directions:

Step 1:

In a pot, medium heat, add oil, onion, and garlic, then sauté 1 minute.

Step 2:

Add tomatoes, sauce, and bay leaf, then simmer (almost boiling, but not at full boil) 15 minutes.

Step 3:

Add oregano and basil, then stir to mix.

Step 4:

Add salt and pepper, to taste, then stir to mix. Simmer (almost boiling, but not at full boil) 5 minutes.

Step 5:

Reduce heat to medium-low. Add browned meatballs. Cover pot with a lid, then simmer for 30 minutes.

Step 6:

Remove bay leaf to discard.

Step 7:
Serve spaghetti noodles with sauce and meatballs on top and with garlic bread on the side.

Fresh Storage:
Cover spaghetti with plastic wrap / film or place in a plastic sealable container and store in the refrigerator. Reheat in a pot. Use within 5 days.

Frozen Storage:
Do NOT freeze.

Your Notes:

_____

_____

MOVIE EIGHT

Course #3: Zabaglione (Italian Custard Dessert)

Ingredients:

4 eggs, separated, keep yolks only

4 Tbsp sugar

1/2 cup Prosecco (Italian sparkling wine, seek
recommendations for a quality choice for your
grocery area)

20 fresh strawberries, cored

Equipment:

a bain marie / a double boiler / OR a metal mixing bowl
with a rim that is bigger around than a pot so that
the bowl can sit on top of the pot and allow the
bottom of the bowl to rest just above the water
level in the pot.

4 individual clear, colorless, glass dessert-sized bowls,
goblets, martini glasses, or parfait glasses

Directions:

Step 1:

In the metal bowl, add yolks and sugar, then whisk, until pale and creamy.

Step 2:

Continuing to whisk, add Prosecco gradually, whisking to mix. Set aside.

Step 3:

In a pot, medium heat, add water, about 1" deep, until just below where metal bowl will rest when placed on top of the pot.

Step 4:

When water begins to boil, reduce heat to a simmer (almost boiling but not at full boil), place metal bowl over the pan of water, then whisk constantly, until egg mixture increases in volume by approximately 5-10 times its original size.

Step 5:
Remove from heat, pour in equal portions into 4 individual serving glass pieces.

Step 6:
Cover each with plastic wrap / film, then transfer to refrigerator to chill, at least 2 hours.

Step 7:
Serve with fresh strawberries on top or on the side.

Fresh Storage:
Cover with plastic wrap / film and store in the refrigerator. Use within 3 days.

Frozen Storage:
Do NOT freeze.

Your Notes:

_____

Round One Guess As to the Inspirational Movie:

_____

MOVIE EIGHT

Level One Hint:

- The inspired dish will make you want to kiss someone and/or will remind you to keep a collar on your beloved dog.

Round Two Guess As to the Inspirational Movie:

_____

MOVIE EIGHT

Level Two Hints:

- Bella Notte is the iconic, romantic sequence from the inspirational 1955 movie, which was almost cut by the director.
- At one Christmas, the protagonist receives a special food gift from Aunt Sarah.
- For a romantic dinner, use an empty wine bottle for a candle holder, have the Tony and Joe play and sing, and share a plate.
- Tony's Restaurant has a special entrance for the protagonist's love interest.

Round Three Guess As to the Inspirational Movie:

MOVIE EIGHT

Level Three Hints:

- Spaghetti & Meatballs served with Marinara Sauce & with Garlic Bread
- On Christmas, 1909, Jim Dear gives Darling a puppy in a hat box, beginning this animated classic on a note similar to a real event in Walt Disney's life.
- The love interest of the protagonist character offers foreshadowing advice about what happens when a baby moves in to a house.
- Si and Am are two matching mischievous characters with blue eyes, who sing a song while making a mess of the house and getting the protagonist into trouble.
- Jock and Trusty make wonderful friends for the protagonist and later for her extended family.

Round Four Guess As to the Inspirational Movie:

_____

MOVIE NINE

Course #1: Tortilla Soup

Ingredients:

16 oz boneless and skinless chicken meat

1/4 tsp salt

1/8 tsp ground black pepper

1 tsp olive oil

1/3 cup vegetable oil

6 corn 6" tortillas, cut into 1/2" strips

1 cup yellow onion, chopped

4 tsp garlic, peeled, smashed, minced

1 Tbsp paprika

2 tsp ground cumin

1 tsp ground coriander

1 tsp chili powder

3 cups chicken stock / broth

3 cups canned plain tomatoes in thick puree

1 bay leaf

2 & 1/2 tsp salt

1/4 cup fresh cilantro, stemmed and chopped

1 avocado, pitted, peeled, cut into 1/2" cubes

1 cup cheddar cheese, grated

1 lime, cut into 4 wedges

Directions:

Step 1:

Preheat oven to 350 degrees.

Step 2:

Lightly coat baking pan with nonstick cooking oil spray.

Step 3:

To prepared pan, add chicken meat. Sprinkle to add salt and pepper. Drizzle to add olive oil.

Step 4:

Place baking pan in preheated oven, on middle rack. Bake for 30-45 minutes, until internal temperature reaches 180 degrees on your thermometer.

Step 5:

Transfer baking pan to a heat-safe surface, such as your stovetop. Set aside 15 minutes to cool.

Step 6:
Transfer chicken to a cutting board, then using 2 total forks, place 1 fork in each hand. Use the 1 fork to hold the chicken in place, then use the other fork to scrape away layers of chicken in strands, making all pieces into shredded chicken. Set aside.

Step 7:
Layer 3 paper towels on a plate. Set aside.

Step 8:
In a deep pan or pot, medium-high heat, add vegetable oil and tortilla strips, then fry, until golden-brown colored on the bottom side.

Step 9:
Flip strips over, then fry, until golden-brown colored on the bottom side.

Step 10:
Remove with a slotted spoon and transfer to prepared plate. Set aside.

Step 11:
Drain out the oil, then return the pan to the hot burner.

Step 12:
Reduce heat to medium, add onion, then cook for 2 minutes.

Step 13:
Add garlic, paprika, cumin, coriander, and chili powder, then stir to mix well and cook for another 3 minutes.

Step 14:
Add chicken stock, tomatoes, bay leaf, salt, and 1/4 of the fried tortilla strips, then bring to boil and then reduce heat until at simmer (almost boiling, but not at full boil). Simmer, uncovered, for 20 minutes.

Step 15:
Remove bay leaf and add cilantro and chicken, then stir to mix well and simmer for 5 minutes.

Step 16:
Add avocado, then stir to mix well.

Step 17:
Remove from the heat, transfer to heat-safe surface, such as a cold stovetop burner.

Step 18:
Portion equal amounts of soup into 4 bowls.

Step 19:
To each bowl, sprinkle to add an equal amount of remaining tortilla strips and cheese.

Step 20:
Squeeze a lime wedge over each bowl, then add the used wedge to each bowl.

Fresh Storage:

Cover with plastic wrap / film or place in a plastic sealable container and store in the refrigerator. Reheat in a pan. Use within 5 days. If you plan to store soup, then do not complete Step 14, or else your strips will be soggy and your cheese will be clumped.

Frozen Storage:
Do NOT freeze.

Your Notes:

_____

_____

MOVIE NINE

Course #2: Fish Tacos served with Mango & Banana Salsa

Tortillas: Frequently Used Side Item Recipes

Mango & Banana Salsa Ingredients:

1 cup mango, peeled, cut fruit away from core, diced 1/4" cubes
1 cup bananas, peeled and diced 1/4" cubes
1 jalapeño, seeded and minced
1 red bell pepper, seeded and diced 1/8" pieces
1/2 bunch cilantro, removed stems and chopped
1/2 red onion, diced 1/8"
2 Tbsp lime juice
salt, to taste

Mango & Banana Salsa Directions:

Step 1:
In a bowl, add mango, banana, jalapeño, pepper, cilantro, onion, and lime juice, then stir to mix well.

Step 2:

Add salt, to taste, then stir to mix well.

Step 3:

Cover with plastic wrap / film. Transfer to refrigerator to chill for at least 1 hour.

Fresh Storage:

Cover salsa with plastic wrap / film or place in a plastic sealable bag and store in the refrigerator. Use within 3 days.

Frozen Storage:

Do NOT freeze.

Fish Tacos Ingredients:

1/4 cup vegetable oil

1 lime, juiced

2 tsp ancho chili powder

4 tilapia, cod, or whiting 6 oz fillets

1 Tbsp olive oil

2 cups dark leafy greens, shredded

1/2 cup red onion, diced

1 avocado, pitted, peeled, and diced 1/4"

Fish Taco Directions:

Step 1:

In a baking pan, add vegetable oil, lime juice, and chili powder, then whisk to mix well.

Step 2:

Add fish fillets in a single layer, then flip fillets and return to a single layer.

Step 3:

Cover with plastic wrap / film. Transfer to refrigerator to marinate for 30 minutes.

Step 4:

In a pan, medium heat, add olive oil and fish fillets, then cook 4 minutes on 1 side.

Step 5:

Flip fish, then cook 4 minutes on other side.

Step 6:

Check each fish fillet by using a fork to gently pull back on a small area on the thickest part of each fillet to make sure it separates into flakes and is colored white all the way through. If a fillet does not pass the test, then cook a few more minutes and recheck.

Step 7:

Transfer cooked fish to a cutting board. Cut fillets into 1" pieces.

Step 8:

Retrieve a tortilla and place on a plate.

Step 9:

Add to the center of the tortilla a portion of fish, a portion of salsa, a portion of shredded greens, a portion of onion, and a portion of avocado.

Step 10:

Fold up the edge of the tortilla closest to you, then fold up the 2 side edges until these overlap.

Step 11:
Repeat Steps 8 - 10 for remaining tortillas.

Fresh/Frozen Storage:
Do NOT store.

Your Notes:

_____

_____

MOVIE NINE

Course #3: Apricot Flan

Ingredients:
4 ceramic 6 oz ramekins
4 Tbsp apricot jam
3/4 cups whole (3%) dairy milk
1/2 cup dairy "half-and- half"
1/2 tsp vanilla extract
1/4 cup sugar
3 eggs, separated and only yolks kept
fine-mesh strainer

Directions:
Step 1:
Preheat oven to 350 degrees.

Step 2:
Place 1 Tbsp jam in each of 4 ramekins. Set aside.

Step 3:
In a pot, low heat, add milk, half-and-half, vanilla extract, and sugar, then whisk to mix well.

Step 4:
Increase heat to medium, then bring to simmer (almost boiling, but not at full boil).

Step 5:
While the pot is simmering, in a bowl, add eggs, then whisk, until light and creamy.

Step 6:
Continuing to whisk, very slowly drizzle to add the simmering mix. Note: If you add the hot mixture too fast, then your eggs will "scramble".

Step 7:
Pour the mixture through a fine-mesh strainer into another bowl.

Step 8:
Pour custard mixture equally into 4 prepared ramekins.

Step 9:

Transfer 4 ramekins into a baking pan with space left around each. Add water into the baking pan until comes up 2" on the outer side of the ramekins. This creates a "water bath" for the custard.

Step 10:

Place the baking pan with water and ramekins set into the preheated oven, on the middle rack. Bake for 40 minutes.

Step 11:

Check flan for doneness by gently jiggling the dish to see if flan just wobbles slightly.

Step 12:

Remove dish set from the oven and place on a heat-safe surface, such as your stovetop. Remove flans from baking pan, place on a wire rack for 10 minutes to cool.

Step 13:
Insert a thin-blade knife along the inner edge of a ramekin. "Run" the knife all along the inner edge to separate the flan from the ramekin edges. Invert the ramekin over a dessert plate, allowing the flan to leave the ramekin.

Step 14:
Repeat Step 13 for remaining 3 ramekins.

Fresh Storage:
Cover with plastic wrap / film and store in the refrigerator. Use within 3 days.

Frozen Storage:
Do NOT freeze.

Your Notes:

_____

_____

Round One Guess As to the Inspirational Movie:

_____

MOVIE NINE

Level One Hint:

- The inspired dish is made by a semi-retired master Chef who has lost his sense of taste/smell but who knows how to use food to welcome a nervous gentleman who has come to dinner with one of his daughters and prattles on about toppings for this dish.

Round Two Guess As to the Inspirational Movie:

_____

MOVIE NINE

Level Two Hints:

- The female protagonist role is split among three daughters, who are drawn to their father's elaborate and colorful dinner table on Sundays to make announcements, fight, sing, and break dishes.
- The father / Chef saves the day for a catering project with his creation of Mexican bread pudding called Bella Mélange, even though he must use the taste and smell of his Chef partner, Gomez, to test his work for excellence.
- Carmen finishes the movie with her career change to becoming the restaurant owner and Chef of Nuevo Latino.
- Martin trades lunches with April as her mother does not have time for making yummy lunches.

Round Three Guess As to the Inspirational Movie:

MOVIE NINE

Level Three Hints:

- Tortilla Soup

- "Perhaps, Perhaps, Perhaps" by Lila Downs is sung and danced to by the three daughters as they work through their issues between them and with themselves as they seek their own paths in their evolving womanhood.

- One of the female protagonists receives love letters from an anonymous interest, and the students who faked the letters end up creating an opportunity that turns into a real relationship.

- Martin's choice for a new wife surprises the woman's mother, who had thought she would be the choice.

- This movie has roots in another movie, although that movie had an Asian background.

Round Four Guess As to the Inspirational Movie:

MOVIE TEN

Course #1: Olive Tapenade served on Crostini

Baguette Bread: Frequently Used Side Item Recipes

Ingredients:
1/4 cup Kalamata olives
1/4 cup stuffed green olives
1/8 cup black olives
1 tsp garlic, peeled, smashed, and minced
1 Tbsp capers
2 basil leaves, rolled into a tube and cut into very fine
    strips (to "chiffonade")
1 Tbsp lemon juice
2 Tbsp extra virgin olive oil
Baguette Bread, sliced into 1" thick pieces
2 Tbsp olive oil

Directions:
Step 1:
In a blender or food processor, add all olives, garlic, capers, lemon juice, and extra virgin olive oil.

Step 2:

Pulse until roughly chopped OR pulse until in a paste (your preference).

Step 3:

Transfer mixture to a bowl. Add basil, then stir to mix well.

Step 4:

Cover bowl with plastic wrap / film. Transfer to refrigerator to chill at least 2 hours.

Step 5:

Using a pastry brush, brush olive oil onto a slice of bread. Set aside.

Step 6:

Repeat Step 5 for all remaining bread slices.

Step 7:

Turning oven broiler on, high setting.

Step 8:
Transfer bread slices to upper wire rack or broiler pan, then toast the slices, until golden-brown colored.

Step 9:
Remove crostini from oven/broiler. Transfer crostini to a serving tray / plate.

Step 10:
To a slice of crostini, spread on 1 Tbsp of olive tapenade.

Step 11:
Repeat Step 10 for all remaining pieces of crostini.

Fresh/Frozen Storage:
Do NOT store.

Your Notes:

_____

_____

MOVIE TEN

Course #2: Timpano

Marinara Sauce Ingredients:
1 Tbsp olive oil
1/2 yellow onion, diced
2 tsp garlic, peeled, smashed, and minced
16 oz canned plain diced tomatoes
16 oz canned plain tomato sauce
1 bay leaf
2 tsp oregano
1 tsp basil
salt, to taste
ground black pepper, to taste

Marinara Directions:
Step 1:
In a pot, medium heat, add oil, onion, and garlic, then sauté 1 minute, constantly stirring.

Step 2:
Add tomatoes, sauce, and bay leaf, then simmer (almost boiling, but not at full boil) 15 minutes.

240

Step 3:
Add oregano and basil, then stir to mix.

Step 4:
Add salt and pepper, to taste, then stir to mix. Simmer (almost boiling, but not at full boil) 5 minutes.

Step 5:
Reduce heat to medium-low. Cover pot with a lid, then simmer for 30 minutes.

Step 6:
Remove bay leaf. Set aside.

Penne Pasta Ingredients:
3 cups dried penne pasta
salt

Penne Pasta Directions:
Step 1:
In a pot, add 3 quarts of water and bring to boil. Add salt, until water is distinctly salty in flavor.

Step 2:
Add penne pasta, then cook according to box directions, until al dente.

Step 3:
Strain pasta out of the water immediately. Run cold water over the penne to stop the cooking process. Set aside.

Sweet Italian Sausage Ingredients:
32 oz sweet Italian sausage links

Sweet Italian Sausage Directions:
Step 1:
Cut links into 1" pieces.

Step 2:
In a pan, medium heat, add sausages pieces, cover with a lid, then cook 8 minutes.

Step 3:
Flip pieces, recover with a lid, then cook another 8 minutes, until done. Set aside.

Hard-Boiled Eggs Ingredients:

6 eggs

Hard-Boiled Eggs Directions:

Step 1:

In a pot, add eggs and enough water to cover the eggs plus be 1" extra over those.

Step 2:

Turn burner on to high heat and bring water to boil.

Step 3:

Cover pot with a lid, remove from heat and set aside for 12 minutes.

Step 4:

Drain hot water from eggs, then run cold water over eggs, until cooled.

Step 5:

Peel eggs, rinse with water, then cut each egg into 6 pieces. Set aside.

Pasta Shell Ingredients:

2 cups flour

1/4 tsp salt

3 eggs, beaten

2 Tbsp olive oil

Pasta Shell Directions:

Step 1:

In a bowl, add flour and the salt, then stir well.

Step 2:

Add eggs and oil, then stir, until the dough forms a ball.
Set aside.

Step 3:

Sprinkle flour on a flat, clean, dry work surface.

Step 4:

Knead the dough for 5-7 minutes, until smooth.

Step 5:

Wrap in plastic wrap / film and set aside on countertop
for 30 minutes.

Step 6:

On the floured work surface, using a rolling pin, press down and roll out from the center of the dough ball, over and over, each time rolling in a different direction, until you roll out a 1/16" circle of even thickness.

Step 7:

With a little wax paper wadded up, coat a 3 quart glass, ceramic, or metal bowl with 2 Tbsp olive oil.

Step 8:

Gently mold the pasta sheet inside the bowl, there should be extra hanging over the edges. Set aside.

Timpano Final Assembly Extra Ingredients:

1 lb mozzarella, cut 1" cubes

1/2 cup Parmigianino cheese, grated

1/2 lb Genoa salami, sliced 1/8" thin

3 Tbsp olive oil

Timpano Assembly Directions:

Step 1:

Preheat oven to 350 degrees.

Step 2:
Into the cooked penne pasta, add 2 cups of the marinara sauce, then stir well.

Step 3:
1st bowl layer: Into the pasta shell lined bowl, add 1 cup of the coated penne into the lined bowl. Add 1/2 cup marinara sauce, 1/3 of the eggs, 1/2 of the sausages, 1/3 of the mozzarella, and 1/2 of the parmesan.

Step 4:
2nd bowl layer: Add 2 cups of the coated penne. Add 1 cup of marinara, the rest of the eggs, the rest of the sausages, 1/3 of the mozzarella, and the rest of the parmesan.

Step 5:
3rd layer: Add all of the remaining penne, all the remaining marinara, all of the salami, and all the remaining marinara.

Step 6:

Fold the overhanging edges of the pasta over the top of the layers to create a cover. Don't double layer the pasta shell, so if you have excess dough, cut it away and discard it.

Step 7:

With a pastry brush, lightly coat the top of the dough shell cover with 1 Tbsp olive oil.

Step 8:

Loosely cover the Timpano with heavy-duty aluminum foil, creating a "tent" over the pasta shell, so that the foil does not touch the pasta shell.

Step 9:

Place the Timpano in the preheated oven, on the middle rack. Bake for 45 minutes.

Step 10:

Remove foil and bake for an additional 45 minutes. Check top with knife, if steam is released, then it is done.

Step 11:

Turn bowl over onto a cutting surface and leaving the bowl on top, set aside for 15 minutes. Remove bowl, cut into wedges as if a piece.

Fresh Storage:

Cover with plastic wrap / film and store in the refrigerator. Reheat in a pan. Use within 3 days.

Frozen Storage:

Do NOT freeze.

Your Notes:

_____

_____

MOVIE TEN

Course #3: Strawberry Ice Cream

Ingredients:

2 cups dairy heavy whipping cream

1/2 cup powdered sugar

1 tsp vanilla extract

1 cup fresh strawberries, cored and mashed

4 fresh strawberries, cored

Directions:

Step 1:

Place a baking pan in the freezer for 30 minutes.

Step 2:

In a bowl, add heavy cream, sugar, vanilla extract, and mashed strawberries, then mix well.

Step 3:

Pour mixed into the chilled baking pan

Step 4:

Cover with plastic wrap / film and place in freezer for at least 3 hours, stir every 30 minutes.

Step 5:

Scoop equal portions of ice cream into clear, colorless, glass dessert-sized bowls, goblets, martini glasses, or parfait glasses.

Step 6:

Garnish each ice cream portion with a fresh strawberry. *Decorative strawberry, cut equally spaced thin slices starting from the larger end and stopping 1/8" from the pointed end, then "fan" out the berry and lay on its side.

Fresh Storage:
Do NOT fresh store.

Frozen Storage:
Cover dish with plastic wrap / film and store in freezer. Remove from freezer. May be frozen up to 4 weeks.

Your Notes:

_____

Round One Guess As to the Inspirational Movie:

_____

MOVIE TEN

Level One Hint:

- The inspired dish causes Pascal, the owner of the restaurant across the street, to talk about killing Primo, the Chef and co-owner of Paradise, for making this particular dish so well.

Round Two Guess As to the Inspirational Movie:

_____

MOVIE TEN

Level Two Hints:

- The Chef protagonist talks about how knowing about food relates to knowing God and angels.
- The maître d` protagonist is the Chef's brother, and he has to explain to customers about why spaghetti does not automatically include meatballs and why risotto is not served with spaghetti.
- The Chef protagonist serves Northern Italian food that is not well known in 1951 and drinks grappa with his friend, a barber.
- In a conversation between the brothers, one says the same response three times about food being the most important part of any restaurant.

Round Three Guess As to the Inspirational Movie:

MOVIE TEN

Level Three Hints:

- Timpano
- Released in 1996, this film set in 1951 on the New Jersey Shore was honored with the New York Film Critics Circle Award and the Boston Society of Film Critics Award for Best New Director and as winners of the Independent Spirit Award for Best First Screenplay.
- Secondo decides to spend the last of their money in hopes of impressing the famous Louis Prima.
- Secondo keeps his love alive of the American dream's possibilities with a test drive of a Cadillac.
- Pascal advises Secondo to bite into life, although Pascal's description fits himself more than it fits Secondo.

Round Four Guess As to the Inspirational Movie:

MOVIE ELEVEN

Course #1: Cucumber Salad

Ingredients:

3 cups cucumbers, sliced thinly

1/3 cup radish, sliced thinly

1/2 cup red onion, sliced thinly

1 tsp salt

1/2 cup sour cream

4 tsp white vinegar

1/8 tsp ground black pepper

1 & 1/2 Tbsp fresh dill, chopped

Directions:

Step 1:

In a bowl, add cucumber, radish, onion, and salt, then mix well.

Step 2:

Set aside for 1 hour, then drain liquid from bowl.

Step 3:
Add sour cream, vinegar, pepper, and dill, then stir to mix
well.

Step 4:
Cover with plastic wrap / film. Transfer bowl to
refrigerator for at least 1 hour.

Fresh Storage:
Cover with plastic wrap / film and store in the
refrigerator. Use within 3 days.

Frozen Storage:
Do NOT freeze.

Your Notes:

_____

_____

MOVIE ELEVEN

Course #2: Beef Bourguignon

Ingredients:

4 oz bacon, chopped

1/4 cup flour

1 & 1/2 lbs well-trimmed boneless beef chuck, cut
    into 1 & 1/2" cubes

1 cup pearl onions

2 cups white button mushrooms, sliced

1/2 cup carrots, sliced 1" pieces

3 tsp garlic, peeled, smashed, and minced

2 tsp canned plain tomato paste

3 cups beef stock / broth

1 bottle red Burgundy wine

2 tsp fresh thyme, chopped

Directions:

Step 1:

In a pot, medium heat, cook bacon until done.

Step 2:

Remove bacon, leaving fat in the pot. Set aside.

Step 3:

In a bowl, add flour and beef, then move beef pieces around in flour until all are coated on all sides.

Step 4:

Transfer floured beef to pot in the bacon fat, medium heat, brown beef.

Step 5:

Flip beef and brown the other side.

Step 6:

Remove browned beef and set aside in a fresh bowl.

Step 7:

Keep the pot on medium heat, add onions, mushrooms, and carrots, then cook for 7 - 10 minutes, until onion begins to develop golden color.

Step 8:

Add garlic and tomato paste, then stir to mix well.

Step 9:

Add beef stock , wine, and thyme. Increase heat to medium-high, bring to simmer (almost boiling but not at full boil).

Step 10:

Reduce heat to maintain simmer for 2 hours, uncovered.

Step 11:

When done, sauce should be thickened and the beef should be very tender. Add salt and pepper, to taste.

Note: This dish is traditionally served as just a stew but may be served over, potatoes, rice, noodles, or with bread, if you prefer.

Fresh Storage:

Cover with plastic wrap / film or place in a plastic sealable container and store in the refrigerator. Reheat in a pan. Use within 5 days.

Frozen Storage:

Cover dish with plastic wrap / film or place in a plastic sealable container, and store in freezer. Remove from freezer and place in refrigerator to thaw before use. Reheat in a pan. May be frozen up to 4 weeks.

Your Notes:

_____

_____

MOVIE ELEVEN

Course #3: Italian Crème Cake with Italian Buttercream Frosting

Cake Ingredients:

1/2 cup butter, softened by sitting out at room temperature

1/2 cup vegetable shortening ("Crisco")

2 cups sugar

5 eggs, separated, keeping yolks (put whites in another bowl to use later in recipe)

2 cups cake flour

1 tsp baking soda

1 cup dairy buttermilk

1 tsp vanilla extract

1 cup sweetened flake coconut

1 cup walnuts, chopped finely

5 eggs, separated, kept whites (from earlier in recipe)

3 round 9" cake pans

parchment paper

Cake Directions:

Step 1:

Lightly coat 3 round 9" cake pans with non-stick vegetable cooking oil spray.

Step 2:

Place a round cake pan onto parchment paper, then use a pencil to trace around the pan.

Step 3:

Repeat tracing until 3 circles have been made on the paper(s).

Step 4:

Using kitchen scissors / shears, cut parchment paper just inside of the traced line so as to avoid having any pencil mark on the circles when done being cut out. Use scissors that are only used in the kitchen for food use; do not use household scissors.

Step 5:

Place a parchment paper circle into each cake pan. Lightly coat parchment paper circles with non-stick vegetable cooking oil spray.

Step 6:
Preheat oven to 350 degrees.

Step 7:
In a mixing bowl, add butter and shortening, then using hand or stand mixer, on medium speed, beat, until mixed well.

Step 8:
Add sugar, then beat, until smooth.

Step 9:
Add egg yolks, then beat, until mixed well. Set aside.

Step 10:
In a bowl, add cake flour and baking soda, then stir to mix well.

Step 11:
Add 1/3 of the flour to the mixing bowl contents, then on medium speed, beat, until mixed well.

Step 12:
Add 1/3 of the buttermilk, beat, until mixed well.

Step 13:
Repeat Steps 11 & 12, until all flour and all buttermilk is mixed in well.

Step 14:
Add vanilla extract, coconut, and walnuts, then stir with a spoon / spatula, until mixed well. Set aside.

Step 15:
In a clean mixing bowl, add egg whites, then using a hand or stand mixer with clean beaters, on high speed, beat egg whites to "stiff peaks".

Checking for stiff peaks:
Stiff peaks are formed when you quickly dip the mixing beaters in and out once, pulling up some of the mixture into a peak, then it stays in the peak shape and does not fall down – like the topping of a meringue pie.

Step 16:
Transfer meringue to other mixing bowl contents, then carefully fold, until mixed.

Step 17:

Divide cake batter equally among 3 prepared cake pans. If batter is not level, then use a spatula or spoon to level.

Step 18:

Place 3 baking pans into preheated oven, on the middle rack. Bake 15 minutes.

Step 19:

Rotate pans front to back and side to side to ensure even baking, then bake another 15-20 minutes.

Step 20:

Check at the center of each of the cakes, with a toothpick inserted straight down and for approximately 3/4 the length of the toothpick, then wiggle the toothpick a bit to make a hole large enough to not scrape the edges of the toothpick as it is removed. If done, then the toothpick should be "clean" or dry after removed, without wet batter sticking to it. (If not "clean", then bake a few minutes more and recheck. Repeat until "clean".)

?

Step 21:
Remove pans when cakes have tested "clean", then place cake pans on wire racks to cool for 10 minutes.

Step 22:
Insert a thin-blade knife along the inner edge of a cake pan. "Run" the knife all along the inner edge to separate the cake from the pan edges. Invert the pan over the wire rack, allowing the cake to leave the pan.

Step 23:
Carefully, peel off the parchment circle and discard it.

Step 24:
Repeat Step 22 & 23 for the other 2 cakes.

Step 25:
Set aside for at least 15 minutes at room temperature, until cool enough to frost.

Italian Buttercream Frosting Ingredients:

2 cups sugar

4 oz warm water (80-100 degrees)

1 cup egg whites (about 8 eggs worth), separated,
  keeping whites only

1/8 tsp salt

1 & 1/4 lbs butter, softened by setting out at room
  temperature

1 Tbsp vanilla extract

Italian Buttercream Frosting Directions:

Step 1:

In a pot, medium-high heat, add sugar and water, then bring to boil. (Start Step 2 now, as timing needs to come together on Step 1's heated sugar and Step 2's whipped egg whites.) Continue to cook, until 244 degrees on your thermometer.

Step 2:

In a mixing bowl with a hand or stand mixer, medium speed, add egg whites and salt, then beat to soft peaks. , whip the whites and salt on medium speed of your stand mixer or hand mixer to "soft peaks", ending on medium-low speed.

This is a timing issue, so adjust the speed of the mixer up or down as you try to get your whites to the perfect consistency at the same time your sugar reaches 244 degrees.

Checking for peaks:
Soft peaks are formed when you quickly dip the mixing beaters in and out once, pulling up some of the mixture into a peak but having it fall back down immediately into the rest of the mixture.

Step 3:
When the hot sugar is at 244 degrees, quickly remove the thermometer from the pan, and quickly transfer the pan to the area next to the mixer. With mixer still on medium-low speed, gently drizzle a slow stream of hot syrup into the mixing bowl, making sure to only pour it along the inside wall of the bowl, not allowing the hot syrup to touch the beaters. Slowly drizzle in all of the syrup.

Attention:

Hot sugar syrup can splatter and spit out of the bowl and onto you, so protect yourself and anyone else in the area. It is advisable to wear a long-sleeved shirt during this process and to keep your face back as far as possible.

Step 4:

Increase mixer speed to high, then beat until mixture is cooled and holds "firm peaks".

Checking for peaks:

Stiff peaks are formed the same way but stay in the peak shape and do not fall down – like the topping of a meringue pie.

Step 5:

Decrease mixing speed to medium. Add butter, 2 Tbsp (or 1 oz) at a time, mixing well in between, until all butter has been added and mixed.

Step 6:
Add vanilla extract, then mix well.

Step 7:
If something looks like it has gone awry, like it is soup, then keep mixing, until it is frosting is fluffy.

Step 8:
Place 1 cooled cake layer on a serving plate or cake stand.

Step 9:
Using a frosting "knife" (rounded tip and not sharp) OR a frosting/pastry spatula, place a large dollop (about 1/4 cup) of frosting in the middle of the top of the cake layer.

Step 10:
Using frosting knife, stay in touch with the frosting to spread it from the middle to cover the cake layer to the edges. Do not touch the cake surface directly with the frosting knife. Make the frosting fairly level, adding more frosting if needed.

Note:

The first frosting is considered as a "crumb coat": a thin layer of frosting meant to keep crumbs from getting in the final frosting layer, so do not worry if this thin layer has crumbs mixed in – it will be covered later.

Note:

Frosting for a 3 layer cake should be divided in 5 equal parts. 1/5 goes between the bottom and middle layers. 1/5 goes between the middle and top layers. 1/5 goes over the top layer. 2/5 goes on the sides of the 3 layers.

Step 11:

Place the second cake layer on the first, then repeat Step 9 & 10 to frost a crumb coat on the top of it.

Step 12:

Place the third cake layer on top, then repeat Steps 9 & 10 to frost a crumb coat on the top of it.

Step 13:

Place several smaller dollops of frosting at equally spaced intervals on the edges of the top layer.

Step 14:
Use these dollops to pull frosting down the sides of the cake, still keeping the frosting knife only in contact with frosting as you move around and combining areas to fully cover the side of the cake all around.

Step 15:
Set aside for 5 minutes to allow the crumb coat to "set".

Step 16:
Place all remaining frosting on the top of the cake, then using frosting knife, spread the final coat of frosting on the top and sides of the cake, until evenly spread.

Fresh Storage:
Cover loosely with plastic wrap / film or place a plastic or glass "dome" over the cake and store in the refrigerator. You can use toothpicks inserted in just far enough to keep toothpicks upright, then "tent" the plastic wrap / film overtop to keep it from touching the cake and disturbing the frosting. Use within 3 days.

Frozen Storage:
Do NOT freeze.

Your Notes:

_____

_____

Round One Guess As to the Inspirational Movie:

_____

MOVIE ELEVEN

Level One Hint:

- The female protagonist took two attempts to make the inspired dish correctly, while she was first trying to impress the editor of a famous cookbook and then when she decided to continue her project.

Round Two Guess As to the Inspirational Movie:

_____

MOVIE ELEVEN

Level Two Hints:

- Both female protagonists enjoy making dinner for their husbands as well as describing the meals to them.
- 365 days and 524 recipes
- Le Cordon Bleu is still a famous culinary school, and while you can still attend the original school in Paris, now you can also attend satellite culinary schools around the world.
- In Paris in the 1950's, a woman taking formal culinary schooling classes was a strange and bold adventure, even for an American diplomat's wife.

Round Three Guess As to the Inspirational Movie:

_____

MOVIE ELEVEN

Level Three Hints:

- Beef (Bouef) Bourguignon
- Today, a woman blogging about food is more welcome than in a professional kitchen, as most sources offer that men trump women 10:1 as Chefs.
- A blog turned into a book deal, which was adapted, along with an autobiography, into a screenplay for a movie based on two true stories.
- In 2009, set in both NYC and France, this movie won Best Actress from the Golden Globe Awards, the Boston, New York, Oklahoma, San Francisco, Southeastern, Phoenix, and North Texas Film Critics, and the Broadcast Film Critics Association, as well as Best Motion Picture from the Golden Globe Awards.
- Bon Appetit!

Round Four Guess As to the Inspirational Movie:

Lisa Shipley and James Shipley

MOVIE TWELVE

Course #1: Chorizo Stuffed Poblano Peppers

Ingredients:

1 Tbsp olive oil

1/2 cup yellow onion, minced

1 Tbsp garlic, minced

1/2 lb raw Mexican chorizo, removed from casings

1 & 1/2 cups cooked white rice

2 Roma tomatoes, seeded and diced

1/3 cup fresh cilantro, chopped finely

1/3 cup sour cream

1/4 cup mozzarella, grated

salt, to taste

ground black pepper, to taste

4 poblano peppers, cut in half lengthwise and seeded

1 cup pepper-jack cheese, shredded

Directions:

Step 1:

In a pan, on medium heat, add oil and onion, then cook, until the onion is translucent.

Step 2:

Add garlic and chorizo, breaking chorizo into small pieces with a spatula, then cook about 7 minutes, until chorizo cooked through.

Step 3:

Transfer pan contents to a bowl.

Step 4:

Add rice, tomatoes, sour cream, cilantro, and mozzarella cheese , then stir to mix well.

Step 5:

Add salt and pepper, to taste, then stir to mix well.

Step 6:

Place equal portions of mixture into each poblano half, then transfer to a baking sheet.

Step 7:

Top each half with an equal portion of pepper-jack cheese.

Step 8:

Place baking sheet in the preheated oven, on the middle rack. Bake at 350 degrees, 20 - 30 minutes, until cheese is melted.

Fresh Storage:

Cover with plastic wrap / film or place in a plastic sealable bag and store in the refrigerator. Reheat in the oven. Use within 3 days.

Frozen Storage:

Do NOT freeze.

Your Notes:

_____

_____

MOVIE TWELVE

Course #2: Moqueca de Camarão aka Brazilian Shrimp Stew

Ingredients:

1 lb tilapia, each fillet halved on the diagonal

12 oz shrimp, shelled and deveined

1/8 cup fresh lime juice

1 Tbsp smoked paprika

1/2 tsp crushed red Chile flakes

1 tsp salt

1/2 tsp ground black pepper

2 Tbsp palm oil

3 tsp garlic, peeled, smashed, and minced

3 Roma tomatoes, diced

2 red onions, sliced into circles

1 red bell pepper, seeded and sliced into circles

1 orange OR yellow bell pepper, seeded and sliced into circles

14 oz can Hearts of Palm, drained, rinsed with tap water, and sliced thinly

1 cup vegetable stock / broth

8 oz coconut milk

1 tsp salt

optional: 1/2 cup fresh cilantro, stemmed and chopped

Step 1:

In a non-metal bowl, add fish, shrimp, lime juice, paprika, chili flakes, salt, and pepper, then using your bare hands, mix well to evenly coat. Set aside 30 minutes.

Step 2:

In a pot, on medium-high heat, add oil and garlic, then cook for 1 minute.

Step 3:

Add tomatoes, onions, peppers, heart of palm, and fish and shrimp mixture, then stir well.

Step 4:

Add vegetable stock, coconut milk and salt, then stir well.

Step 5:

Reduce heat to medium, then cook for 15 minutes.

Step 6:

Check each fish fillet by using a fork to gently pull back on a small area on the thickest part of each fillet to make sure it separates into flakes and is colored white all the way through. If a fillet does not pass the test, then cook a few more minutes and recheck.

Step 7:

Serve over rice, then (optional) sprinkle to add cilantro.

Fresh Storage:

Cover with plastic wrap / film or place in a plastic sealable bag and store in the refrigerator. Reheat in a pan. Use within 2 days.

Frozen Storage:

Do NOT freeze.

Your Notes:

_____

_____

MOVIE TWELVE

Course #3: Orange Flan

Ingredients:
4 ceramic 6 oz ramekins

4 Tbsp Orange Marmalade

3/4 cups whole (3%) dairy milk

1/2 cup dairy "half-and- half"

1/2 tsp vanilla extract

1/4 cup orange juice

2 Tbsp orange zest

1/4 cup sugar

4 eggs, separated, only yolks kept

Directions:
Step 1:

Preheat oven to 350 degrees.

Step 2:

Place 1 Tbsp marmalade in each of 4 ramekins. Set aside.

Step 3:

In a pot, low heat, add milk, half-and-half, vanilla extract, orange juice, orange zest, and sugar, then whisk to mix well.

Step 4:

Increase heat to medium, then bring to simmer (almost boiling, but not at full boil).

Step 5:

While the pot is simmering, in a bowl, add eggs, then whisk, until light and creamy.

Step 6:

Continuing to whisk, very slowly drizzle to add the simmering mix. Note: If you add the hot mixture too fast, then your eggs will "scramble".

Step 7:

Pour the mixture through a fine-mesh strainer into another bowl.

Step 8:

Pour custard mixture equally into 4 prepared ramekins.

Step 9:

Transfer 4 ramekins into a baking pan with space left around each. Add water into the baking pan until comes up 2" on the outer side of the ramekins. This creates a "water bath" for the custard.

Step 10:

Place the baking pan with water and ramekins set into the preheated oven, on the middle rack. Bake for 40 minutes.

Step 11:

Check flan for doneness by gently jiggling the dish to see if flan just wobbles slightly.

Step 12:

Remove dish set from the oven and place on a heat-safe surface, such as your stovetop. Remove flans from baking pan, place on a wire rack for 10 minutes to cool.

Step 13:
Insert a thin-blade knife along the inner edge of a ramekin. "Run" the knife all along the inner edge to separate the flan from the ramekin edges. Invert the ramekin over a dessert plate, allowing the flan to leave the ramekin.

Step 14:
Repeat Step 13 for remaining 3 ramekins.

Fresh Storage:
Cover with plastic wrap / film and store in the refrigerator. Use within 3 days.

Frozen Storage:
Do NOT freeze.

Your Notes:

_____

_____

Round One Guess As to the Inspirational Movie:

_____

MOVIE TWELVE

Level One Hint:

- The female protagonist teaches Americans how to make this ethnic dish from her country and her passion for a key ingredient, which earns her the attention of a television show producer and a job as a Chef hostess.

Round Two Guess As to the Inspirational Movie:

_____

MOVIE TWELVE

Level Two Hints:

- The female protagonist's most important ingredient is to share the dish with someone you love.
- Some people would not mind dying from a woman cooking with too much butter.
- Chili pepper kisses and red dresses make other women want to wear their hair down too!
- Monica advises that men are like melons in that you have a hard time finding a good one.

Round Three Guess As to the Inspirational Movie:

_____

MOVIE TWELVE

Level Three Hints:

- Moqueca de Camarão aka Brazilian Shrimp Stew
- Yemania, the Brazilian Sea Goddess, receives gifts, curses, and requests.
- Due to the female protagonist's issue with motion sickness, she must always drive in a car, lead while dancing, take the stairs instead of an elevator, and be in a certain position with her sexual partner.
- This comedy film released in 2000 has settings in Brazil and San Francisco, although the entire movie was filmed in Brazil.
- The female protagonist has a television show called The Passion Food, which has a supporting character, Monica, a transsexual, who eventually falls in love with the producer of the show, Cliff.

Round Four Guess As to the Inspirational Movie:

MOVIE THIRTEEN

Course #1: Wild Rice & Mushrooms

Ingredients:

3/4 cup uncooked wild rice

1/4 tsp dried thyme

1/4 tsp dried basil

1 tsp salt

2 cups chicken stock / broth

4 cup white button mushrooms, sliced

1/4 cup butter

1 cup yellow onion, chopped finely

1/2 tsp ground black pepper

Directions:

Step 1:

In a bowl, add rice and cold water (enough to cover the rice), stir, then drain away water.

Step 2:

Repeat Step 1's rinsing process two more times.

Step 3:

In a pot with a lid, add drained rice, thyme, basil, salt, and stock, stir to mix well. Cover and bring to boil.

Step 4:

Reduce heat and simmer (almost boiling, but not a full boil), for 40 minutes. Set aside.

Step 5:

In a pan, on medium heat, add butter and onion, stir to mix well, then cook, until onion is translucent.

Step 6:

Add mushrooms, stir to mix well, then cook, until browned.

Step 7:

Add black pepper, then stir to mix well.

Step 8:

Transfer both the pan contents and the pot contents to a bowl, then add salt and pepper, to taste.

Fresh Storage:

Cover with plastic wrap / film and store in the refrigerator. Reheat in a pan. Use within 3 days.

Frozen Storage:

Do NOT freeze.

Your Notes:

_____

MOVIE THIRTEEN

Course #2: Baked Walleye served with Caramelized Carrots

Walleye Ingredients;
4 walleye 8 oz fillets
1 yellow onion, chopped in rings
4 Tbsp butter
1 tsp salt
1/2 tsp ground black pepper
3 Tbsp lemon juice

Caramelized Carrots Ingredients:
2 cups baby carrots
2 Tbsp butter
1 Tbsp honey
1 tsp salt

Special Equipment:
heavy-duty aluminum foil that is at least 16" wide

Step 1:
Preheat oven to 400 degrees.

Step 2:
Cut heavy-duty aluminum foil into 5 separate 16" x 12" sheets.

Step 3:
Position a sheet so that the 16" side goes from left to right, then fold the sheet in half to create a crease line.

Step 4:
Then unfold that sheet and set aside.

Step 5:
Repeat Steps 3 & 4 for all remaining sheets.

Step 6:
Place a fillet in the middle of the left "half" (from the crease line) of the foil sheet. Gently turn up all 4 edges of foil to make a shallow bowl.

Step 7:

On top of each fillet, add a ring of onion.

Step 8:

Add equal amounts of salt, pepper, butter, and lemon juice.

Step 9:

For 1 fillet foil, fold the right half of the foil over top of the left half, lining up the edges.

Step 10:

Holding both edges together, fold over then pinch all along the edges to seal the fish and toppings into an airtight pouch.

Step 11:

Repeat Steps 9 & 10, until all fillets are in sealed pouches. Note: 1 pouch will be left over.

Step 12:

In the last foil pouch, place carrots, butter, honey, and salt. Fold in the same way and seal in the same way as the fish in Steps 9 & 10.

Lisa Shipley and James Shipley

Step 13:
Place foil pouches on a baking sheet.

Step 14:
Place baking sheet in the preheated oven, on the middle rack. Bake 10-15 minutes. Pouches should expand with steam.

Step 15:
Carefully remove the baking sheet and place on a heat-safe surface, such as your stovetop.

Step 16:
Carefully, transfer each fish pouch to a serving plate.

Step 17:
Carefully open the packet, keeping your face and hands as far away from the packet as steam will release and can burn you.

Step 18:
Carefully open the carrot pouch, again keeping away from the steam, then add equal portions to each plate.

Fresh Storage:
Cover with plastic wrap / film and store in the refrigerator. Reheat in a pan. Use within 1 days.

Frozen Storage:
Do NOT freeze.

Your Notes:

_____

_____

MOVIE THIRTEEN

Course #3: Fry Bread

Ingredients:
4 cups flour
3 Tbsp sugar
4 tsp baking powder
1 tsp salt
1 & 2/3 cup water (80 - 100 degrees)
1/3 cup powdered milk
1/3 cup vegetable oil
2 cups solid vegetable shortening / "Crisco"

Special Note:
This is Chef James' mother's recipe. Enjoy!

Directions:
Step 1:
In a bowl, add flour, sugar, baking powder, salt, water, powdered milk, and oil, then mix with a spoon / spatula to mix well.

Step 2:
Knead 3 to 5 minutes, until smooth. Do not use a mixer.

Step 3:
Break into pieces roughly the size of a deck of cards.

Step 4:
In a cast-iron frying pan (cast iron is best, but another high edged pot or pan will do), on medium heat, bring shortening to about 350 degrees. Adjust heat level to maintain 350 degrees.

Step 5:
Set up a dinner-size plate covered with several paper-towels laying on top to use. Or use a plate covered with a folded brown-paper-bag. Set aside.

Step 6:
Stretch, by hand, 1 piece into an 8" circle.

Step 7:
Gently lower 1 circle of dough into the frying pan, by holding 1 edge and gently laying it down flat. Fry for 1 to 2 minutes, until golden-brown. Use tongs to grasp 1 edge and to flip the circle of dough over. Fry for another 1 to 2 minutes, until golden brown.

Step 8:
Using tongs, grasp 1 edge and transfer fry bread to paper / bag covered plate set up from Step 5 so that the fry bread lays down flat.

Step 9:
Immediately sprinkle it on both sides with either confectioners' (powdered) or granulated white sugar. Then, using tongs, grasp 1 edge and transfer the fry bread to plain serving platter.

Step 10:
Repeat Steps 5 - 9 for each remaining piece of dough, until all dough has been fried. Continue to place new paper towels or bags on the drain plate as needed. Continue to stack finished fry bread on a plain serving platter.

Fresh Storage:

Cover with plastic wrap / film or place in a plastic sealable bag and store in the refrigerator. Reheat in a pan. Use within 3 days.

Frozen Storage:

Cover dish with plastic wrap / film or place in a plastic sealable bag, and store in freezer. Remove from freezer and place on countertop to thaw before use. Reheat in a pan. May be frozen up to 2 weeks.

Your Notes:

_____

_____

Round One Guess As to the Inspirational Movie:

_____

MOVIE THIRTEEN

Level One Hint:

- The inspired dish is made by three different people in the inspirational movie and is used in a story told about feeding 100 people gathered.

Round Two Guess As to the Inspirational Movie:

_____

MOVIE THIRTEEN

Level Two Hints:

- There is one dish which makes any meal special, according to one of the male protagonists.
- Co-author Chef James is especially fond of his childhood memories associated with the inspirational food, and the movie concurs with Chef James in that this inspirational dish is a matter of great pride for those who are known to make it well, especially for large gatherings.
- The inspired dish can be used as a side item, as a foundation for an "Indian Taco", or as a dessert item, depending upon toppings.

Round Three Guess As to the Inspirational Movie:

_____

MOVIE THIRTEEN

Level Three Hints:

- Fry Bread (Native American)
- The inspirational movie is set in Idaho in 1976 and 1998, and it is based upon a book.
- KREZ is a radio station that makes traffic and weather reports.
- Knowing how to tell a story in the oral tradition can earn you a car ride, in reverse gear.
- The film ends with an idea about forgiveness, which can be paramount to a young man in his relationship with his father.

Round Four Guess As to the Inspirational Movie:

_____

MOVIE FOURTEEN

Course #1: Black-Eyed Peas Relish Crudité

Baguette Bread: Frequently Used Side Item Recipes

Ingredients:

16 oz canned black-eyed peas, drained and rinsed well

16 oz canned black beans, drained and rinsed well

16 oz can red kidney beans, drained and rinsed well

3/4 cup (from a jar) chopped pimentos, juice included

1 bunch scallions, green part only, sliced thinly

1 Tbsp fresh oregano, stemmed and chopped

1 Tbsp Tabasco sauce

1 Tbsp Worcestershire sauce

1 tsp ground black pepper

1/2 bunch cilantro, stemmed and chopped

1 jalapeño chili, minced

10 oz canned "mild" Rotel

1 green bell pepper, seeded and diced

2 tsp garlic, peeled, smashed, and minced

1/2 cup olive oil

1/4 cup balsamic vinegar

Directions:

Step 1:
With serrated bread knife, cut baguette into 1/4" slices.

Step 2:
In a bowl, add peas, all beans, pimentos, scallions, oregano, Tabasco, Worcestershire, pepper, cilantro, jalapeño, Rotel, pepper, and garlic, then stir. Set aside.

Step 3:
In a bowl, add balsamic vinegar, then while whisking vigorously and continuously, slowly drizzle in oil to form an emulsion.

Step 4:
Combine bowls, then stir to mix well.

Step 5:
Cover with plastic wrap / film, then transfer to refrigerator for at least 1 hour.

Step 6:
Using a pastry brush, brush olive oil onto a slice of bread. Set aside.

Step 7:

Repeat Step 6 for all remaining bread slices.

Step 8:

Turning oven broiler on, high setting. Transfer bread slices to upper wire rack or broiler pan, then toast the slices, until golden-brown colored.

Step 9:

Remove toast from oven/broiler. Transfer toast to a serving tray / plate.

Step 10:

Remove relish from refrigerator, then spoon onto toast.

Fresh Storage:

Cover unused relish with plastic wrap / film and store in the refrigerator. Use within 5 days.

Frozen Storage:

Do NOT freeze.

Your Notes:

MOVIE FOURTEEN

Course #2: BBQ Beef Brisket

Beef Brisket Ingredients:

4# beef brisket slab

2 tsp ground black pepper

2 tsp salt

1/2 tsp onion powder

1/2 tsp smoked paprika powder

1/2 tsp dry mustard

1/4 tsp cayenne pepper

roasting pan with oven-safe metal rack

Beef Brisket Directions:

Step 1:

Preheat oven to 250 degrees.

Step 2:

Place brisket on a cutting board. Remove all but 1/4" of the fat from the top.

Step 3:
Cut out the thick heel of fat from the underside of the point. Set aside.

Step 4:
In a bowl, add pepper, salt, onion powder, paprika, mustard, and cayenne, then stir to mix well.

Step 5:
Spread rub evenly over brisket, pressing to help it stick.

Step 6:
Place the oven-safe metal rack in the roasting pan. Place brisket on the rack, fat-side up. Cover the pan with a lid or with aluminum foil. If using foil, then "tent" foil so that it does not touch the meat.

Step 7:
Place roasting pan in the preheated oven, on the middle rack. Bake for 8 hours. Do not open the oven during the 8 hours.

Step 8:
Remove lid / foil. Bake for another 45 minutes.

Step 9:
Remove the roasting pan from the oven and place on a heat-safe surface, such as your stovetop, to cook 30 minutes.

Step 10:
Slice meat in the opposite direction from the grain.

Step 11:
Serve sliced brisket with BBQ sauce.

BBQ Sauce Ingredients:
2 qts ketchup

2 qts water

3/4 cup yellow or red onion, peeled and diced

2 tsp dry mustard

1/2 Tbsp red pepper flakes

1 oz concentrated vegetable stock / base OR
    1 vegetable bouillon cube

1/2 Tbsp garlic, peeled, smashed, and minced

1/2 Tbsp chili powder

1/2 Tbsp Seasoning Salt

1 & 3/4 cups any brown sugar

1 & 3/4 cups white vinegar

BBQ Sauce Directions:

Step 1:

In a pot, on medium heat, add ketchup, water, onion, mustard, red pepper flakes, stock/base/bouillon, garlic, chili powder, and seasoning salt, then stir to mix well.

Step 2:

Cook until begins to boil.

Step 3:

Reduce heat to medium-low, then simmer (almost boiling but not at full boil) for 20 minutes.

Step 4:

Add brown sugar and vinegar, then simmer for another 10 minutes.

Step 5:

Serve with sliced brisket.

Fresh Storage:

Place unused BBQ sauce in a plastic sealable bag or container and store in the refrigerator. Reheat in a pan. Use within 2 weeks.

Place meat (with or without sauce on it) in a plastic sealable bag or container and store in the refrigerator. Reheat in a pan. Use within 3 days.

Frozen Storage:

Place unused sauce in a plastic sealable bag or container, and store in freezer. Remove from freezer and place on countertop to thaw before use. Reheat in a pan. May be frozen up to 3 months.

Place meat (with or without sauce) in a plastic sealable bag or container, and store in freezer. Remove from freezer and place in the refrigerator to thaw before use. Reheat in a pan. May be frozen up to 1 month.

Your Notes:

_____

_____

MOVIE FOURTEEN

Course #3: Browned Butter Carrot Cake with Cream Cheese Frosting

Browned Butter Carrot Cake Ingredients:

2 cups pineapple, drained well and chopped into 1/4"
  pieces, then placed in a bowl

3 & 1/2 cups carrot, grated then immediately added to
  pineapple and stirred to mix well, to keep from
  getting brown

2 cups sweetened flake coconut

1 # butter

6 eggs, beaten

2 Tbsp vanilla extract

2 cups flour

1 & 1/2 cups almonds

2 tsp baking powder

2 tsp baking soda

2 tsp cinnamon

1 cup powdered sugar

1 cup brown sugar

4 round 9" cake pans

parchment paper

Browned Butter Carrot Cake Directions:

Step 1:

Lightly coat 4 round 9" cake pans with non-stick vegetable cooking oil spray.

Step 2:

Place a round cake pan onto parchment paper, then use a pencil to trace around the pan. Repeat tracing until 4 circles have been made on the paper(s).

Step 3:

Using kitchen scissors / shears, cut parchment paper just inside of the traced line so as to avoid having any pencil mark on the circles when done being cut out. Use scissors that are only used in the kitchen for food use; do not use household scissors.

Step 4:

Place a parchment paper circle into each cake pan. Lightly coat parchment paper circles with non-stick vegetable cooking oil spray.

Step 5:

Preheat oven to 325 degrees.

Step 6:
Add almonds to a food processor or blender, then using a medium or low speed, grind into very coarse flour texture. Set aside.

Step 7:
In a bowl, add pineapple with carrot and coconut, then stir to mix well. Set aside.

Step 8:
In a pan, on medium heat, brown butter:
butter will melt and separate, begin to turn golden-brown in color, begin to smell like caramel, then form brown "bits" / particles /granules in bottom of the pan.

Step 9:
Occasionally stir and scrape up the browned "bits", to allow more "bits" to form, for 2 minutes, monitoring it constantly to avoid letting it burn*. If you smell a change away from "caramel" to "sharp or burnt", then stop before the 2 minutes. Immediately remove from heat and place on a heat-safe surface, such as a cold burner, cool at room temperature. Do NOT refrigerate!

*Do not used burned butter – just accept that you will need to clean the pan and "do over". No worries!

Step 10:
In a bowl, add flour, ground almonds, baking powder, and baking soda, then whisk to mix well. Set aside.

Step 11:
In a bowl, add cinnamon, powdered sugar, and brown sugar, then stir to mix well.

Step 12:
Add eggs and vanilla extract, then stir to mix well.

Step 13:
Add flour/almond mixture, then stir to mix well, making sure to scrape the bottom of the bowl, until no dry flour shows in the batter.

Step 14:
Add browned butter and browned "bits", then stir to mix through batter.

Step 15:

Add carrot mixture, then stir to mix through batter.

Step 16:

Divide batter equally into the 4 prepared cake pans.
If batter is not level, then use a spatula or spoon to level.

Step 17:

Place 4 baking pans into preheated oven, with 2 pans on
a rack just above the middle and 2 pans on a rack just
below the middle. Bake 13 minutes.

Step 18:

Rotate pans front to back and side to side to ensure
even baking, then bake another 14 minutes.

Step 19:

Check at the center of each of the cakes, with a
toothpick inserted straight down and for approximately
3/4 the length of the toothpick, then wiggle the
toothpick a bit to make a hole large enough to not
scrape the edges of the toothpick as it is removed.

If done, then the toothpick should be "clean" or dry after removed, without wet batter sticking to it. (If not "clean", then bake a few minutes more and recheck. Repeat until "clean".)

Step 20:
Remove pans when cakes have tested "clean", then place cake pans on wire racks to cool for 10 minutes.

Step 21:
Insert a thin-blade knife along the inner edge of a cake pan. "Run" the knife all along the inner edge to separate the cake from the pan edges. Invert the pan over the wire rack, allowing the cake to leave the pan.

Step 22:
Carefully, peel off the parchment circle and discard it.

Step 23:
Repeat Steps 21 & 22 for the other 3 cakes.

Step 24:
Set aside for at least 15 minutes at room temperature, until cool enough to frost.

Cream Cheese Frosting Ingredients:

1 cup butter , softened from setting on a countertop at
    room temperature

2#s cream cheese, softened from setting on a
    countertop at room temperature

5 cups powdered sugar

1 Tbsp vanilla extract

1 lemon, zest in 1 bowl & 2 Tbsp juice in 1 bowl

1 orange, zest in same bowl with lemon zest & 1 Tbsp
    juice in same bowl with lemon juice

Cream Cheese Frosting Directions:

Step 1:

In a mixing bowl, add butter and cream cheese, then using
a hand or standing mixer on medium speed, beat for 5
minutes, until smooth and creamy.

Step 2:

Turn off mixer. Add 1 cup of the powdered sugar, then
turn mixer to low, then beat until mixed through.

Step 3:

Repeat Step 2 until all of the powdered sugar has been
added and mixed through.

Step 4:

Add vanilla extract, juices, and zests, then mix through.

Step 5:

Check frosting consistency to see if makes "stiff peaks".

Checking for stiff peaks:

Quickly dip the mixing beaters in and out once, pulling up some of the mixture into a peak and having it stay in the peak shape and not fall down – like the topping of a meringue pie. Set aside.

Step 6:

Place 1 cooled cake layer on a serving plate or cake stand.

Step 7:

Using a frosting "knife" (rounded tip and not sharp) OR a frosting/pastry spatula, place a large dollop (about 1/4 cup) of frosting in the middle of the top of the cake layer.

Step 8:

Using frosting knife, stay in touch with the frosting to spread it from the middle to cover the cake layer to the edges. Do not touch the cake surface directly with the frosting knife. Make the frosting fairly level, adding more frosting if needed.

Note:

The first frosting is considered as a "crumb coat": a thin layer of frosting meant to keep crumbs from getting in the final frosting layer, so do not worry if this thin layer has crumbs mixed in – it will be covered later.

Note:

Frosting for a 4 layer cake should be divided in 7 equal parts. 1/7 goes between each layer. 1/7 goes over the top layer. 3/7 goes on the sides of the 4 layers.

Step 9:

Place the second cake layer on the first frosted layer, then repeat Steps 7 & 8 to frost a crumb coat on the top it.

Step 10:
Place the third cake layer on top, then repeat Steps 7 & 8 to frost a crumb coat on the top of it.

Step 11:
Place the fourth cake layer on top, then repeat Steps 7 & 8 to frost a crumb coat on the top of it.

Step 12:
Place several smaller dollops of frosting at equally spaced intervals on the edges of the top layer.

Step 13:
Use these dollops to pull frosting down the sides of the cake, still keeping the frosting knife only in contact with frosting as you move around and combining areas to fully cover the side of the cake all around.

Step 14:
Set aside for 5 minutes to allow the crumb coat to "set".

Step 15:
Place all remaining frosting on the top of the cake, then using frosting knife, spread the final coat of frosting on the top and sides of the cake, until evenly spread.

*Cake actually serves 8 people easily and "fresh" stores very well for leftovers. Amazing with a cup of coffee!
Fresh Storage:
Cover loosely with plastic wrap / film or place a plastic or glass "dome" over the cake and store in the refrigerator. You can use toothpicks inserted in just far enough to keep toothpicks upright, then "tent" the plastic wrap / film overtop to keep it from touching the cake and disturbing the frosting. Use within 5 days.

Frozen Storage:
Do NOT freeze.

Your Notes:

_____

Round One Guess As to the Inspirational Movie:

_____

MOVIE FOURTEEN

Level One Hint:

- The inspired dish is discussed several times by the restaurant owner of The Bone Shack.

Round Two Guess As to the Inspirational Movie:

_____

MOVIE FOURTEEN

Level Two Hints:

- The restaurant owner works to perfect his recipe and is finally satisfied when an accidental addition reveals that he needed to add salt.

- One of the patrons of the restaurant is a female protagonist and go-go dancer, and she knows a lot about useless talents.

- The baddies in this inspirational movie are not interested in dining at this restaurant, at least not on the inspired dish.

Round Three Guess As to the Inspirational Movie:

_____

MOVIE FOURTEEN

Level Three Hints:

- BBQ Beef Brisket
- This movie is considered half of a double-feature of full-length feature horror films known as Grindhouse, released in 2007.
- The heroine doctor uses color-coded friends of yellow, blue, and red.
- Zombie movies are popular, and so are girls who have a gun replacing a leg.

Round Four Guess As to the Inspirational Movie:

MOVIE FIFTEEN

Course #1: Cornbread served with

Bacon & Shrimp & Creole Remoulade

Creole Seasoning Ingredients:
* You may also buy a premade Creole seasoning and skip this recipe section.

5 Tbsp sweet paprika

4 Tbsp salt

2 Tbsp onion powder

2 Tbsp garlic powder

2 Tbsp dried oregano leaves

2 Tbsp dried basil

1 Tbsp dried thyme leaves

1 Tbsp ground black pepper

1 Tbsp ground white pepper

1 Tbsp cayenne pepper

1 Tbsp celery seed

Creole Seasoning Directions:
Step 1:
In a food processor/spice grinder, add paprika, salt, onion powder, garlic powder, oregano, basil, thyme, ground black pepper, ground white pepper, cayenne pepper, and celery seed, then process for 5 seconds.

Step 2:
Transfer to covered container or plastic sealable bag. Set aside.

Creole Remoulade Ingredients:
1/4 cup mayonnaise

1 Tbsp Creole mustard

1 Tbsp ketchup

1 tsp Creole seasoning

1 tsp horseradish

1 tsp garlic, peeled, smashed, and minced

1 Tbsp lemon juice

1 tsp capers

1 green onion, chopped

1/4 tsp cayenne pepper

1/4 tsp paprika

1/8 tsp hot sauce

Creole Remoulade Directions:

Step 1:

In a bowl, add mayonnaise, Creole mustard, ketchup, Creole seasoning, horseradish, garlic, lemon juice, capers, green onion, cayenne pepper, paprika, and hot sauce, then stir to mix well.

Step 2:

Cover with plastic wrap / film. Transfer to refrigerator, at least 15 minutes, until ready to use.

Cornbread Ingredients:

1 cup cornmeal
1 cup flour
1/2 tsp baking soda
1/2 tsp salt
1/2 cup butter, melted
1/3 cup sugar
2 eggs
1 cup buttermilk

Cornbread Directions:

Step 1:

Preheat oven to 375 degrees.

Step 2:

Lightly coat an 8 x 8" baking pan with non-stick vegetable oil cooking spray.

Step 3:

In a bowl, add cornmeal, flour, baking soda, and salt, then whisk to mix well. Set aside.

Step 4:

In another bowl, add melted butter and sugar, then stir to mix well. Allow to cool.

Step 5:

Add 1 egg, then stir vigorously with a fork, until mixed well.

Step 6:

Add 2nd egg, then stir vigorously with a fork, until mixed well.

Step 7:
Add the entire bowl of dry ingredients, then add buttermilk on top. **At this point it is very important to not over-mix the dough, so...** using a spatula, gently fold 5-7 times to mix the wet and dry ingredients, carefully scraping the bottom of the bowl on each pass through the dough. Do **not** stir vigorously.

Step 8:
Gently pour mix into the prepared pan, scraping sides of the bowl to get the entire mixture into the pan.

Step 9:
Place the pan into the preheated oven, on the middle rack. Bake for 30 - 35 minutes, until golden-brown colored.

Step 10:
Check at the center of the bread with a toothpick inserted straight down and for approximately 3/4 the length of the toothpick. If done, then the toothpick should be "clean" or dry, without wet batter sticking to it.

Step 11:
Remove baking pan from the oven and place on a heat-safe surface, such as your stovetop. Set aside.

Bacon & Shrimp Ingredients:
20 small shrimp (frozen or fresh), tail off, shelled, and deveined
1 Tbsp Creole seasoning
4 strips thick-cut bacon, diced

Bacon & Shrimp Directions:
Step 1:
In a bowl, add shrimp and seasoning, then stir to coat. Set aside.

Step 2:
In a pan, on medium heat, add diced bacon, then cook 3 minutes.

Step 3:
Add seasoned shrimp, then cook 5 minutes, until cooked through.

Step 4:

Place pan on a heat-safe surface, such as a cold burner. Set aside.

Assembly:

Step 1:

Gather cornbread, Creole remoulade, and serving plates, then place all on countertop near stovetop.

Step 2:

Either arrange for people to self-serve assemble OR On an individual serving plate, add a piece of cornbread. Add a portion of bacon & shrimp, the drizzle to add Creole remoulade.

Step 3:

If doing plating, then repeat Step 2 for 4 plates.

Fresh Storage:

Cover unused cornbread with plastic wrap / film or place in a plastic sealable bag and store in the refrigerator. Reheat in a pan. Use within 5 days.

Cover unused bacon & shrimp mixture with plastic wrap / film or place in a plastic sealable container and store in the refrigerator. Reheat in a pan. Use within 1 day.

Cover unused creole remoulade with plastic wrap / film or place in a plastic sealable container and store in the refrigerator. Use within 5 days.

Place unused creole seasoning in a plastic sealable bag or container and store in dry storage, away from direct sunlight. Use within 3 months.

Frozen Storage:

Do NOT freeze any elements.

Your Notes:

_____

_____

MOVIE FIFTEEN

Course #2: Salmon served with Lemon Crème Fraiche Sauce

Lemon Crème Fraiche Sauce Ingredients:

1 cup crème fraiche

1 Tbsp lemon juice

1 tsp lemon zest

1/4 tsp salt

1/4 tsp ground white pepper

Lemon Crème Fraiche Sauce Directions:

Step 1:

In a bowl, add crème fraiche, lemon juice, lemon zest, salt, and white pepper, then whisk to mix well.

Step 2:

Cover with plastic wrap / film. Transfer to refrigerator, until ready to use.

Salmon Ingredients:

2 Tbsp honey

1/4 tsp salt

1 Tbsp olive oil

2 Tbsp shallot, minced

2 Tbsp lemon juice

1 tsp lemon zest

4 salmon 6-8 oz fillets

Salmon Directions:

Step 1:

In a bowl, add honey, salt, olive oil, shallots, lemon juice, and lemon zest, then whisk to mix well.

Step 2:

Transfer to a sealable plastic bag. Add salmon fillets, then rotate, until salmon coated with mixture. Place bag of marinating salmon into a bowl or pan to catch any possible leaking.

Step 3:

Transfer to refrigerator to chill for 1 hour.

Step 4:
Preheat oven to 400 degrees.

Step 5:
Coat a baking pan with non-stick cooking spray.

Step 6:
Add salmon.

Step 7:
Place pan in preheated oven, on the middle rack, then bake 15 minutes, until done.

Step 8:
Check each salmon fillet by using a fork to gently pull back on a small area on the thickest part of each fillet to make sure it separates into flakes all the way through. If a fillet does not pass the test, then cook a few more minutes and recheck.

Step 9:
Transfer pan to a heat-safe surface, such as your stovetop. Set aside.

Assembly Ingredients:

2 mesclun or salad lettuce mix of choice

1/4 cup dill sprigs, stemmed

1/4 cup fresh tarragon leaves, stemmed

1 Tbsp lemon juice

1 Tbsp extra virgin olive oil

1 lemon, cut into 4 wedges

Assembly Directions:

Step 1:

In a bowl, add mesclun mix, dill, and tarragon, then mix well.

Step 2:

Add lemon juice, then mix well. Add extra virgin olive oil, then mix well.

Step 3:

To an individual dinner plate, add a portion of the salad mix. Add a fillet of salmon on top , then drizzle to add lemon crème fraiche sauce over salmon and salad. Add lemon wedge to the side.

Step 4:

Repeat Step 3 for 3 remaining plates.

Fresh / Frozen Storage:

Do NOT store.

Your Notes:

_____

_____

MOVIE FIFTEEN

Course #3: Blackberry & Peach Cream Crumble

Crust Ingredients:

3 cups graham crackers, crushed into crumbs

4 Tbsp sugar

3/4 cup butter, melted

Crust Directions:

Step 1:

In a bowl, add graham cracker crumbs, sugar, and melted butter, then stir to mix well.

Step 2:

Transfer 1/4 cup of mixture to a bowl, then set aside.

Step 3:

In a 9 x 13" baking pan, add the remaining of the crust mix. Using your hands, press the crumbs into the bottom and sides of the pan, until evenly and firmly packed into a crust.

Step 4:

Transfer pan to refrigerator, until ready to assemble.

Blackberry Ingredients:

3 cups fresh blackberries

1/3 cup sugar

Blackberry Directions:

Step 1:

In a bowl, add blackberries and sugar, then mix well.

Step 2:

Cover with plastic wrap / film. Transfer to refrigerator, until ready to assemble.

Peach Cream Ingredients:

5 peaches, peeled, pitted and sliced thinly

1 & 1/4 oz packet of unflavored gelatin

1/8 cup warm water (80 – 100 degrees)

1 & 1/2 cups powdered sugar

8 oz cream cheese, softened to room temperature

1/2 tsp vanilla extract

2 cups dairy heavy whipping cream

Peach Cream Directions:

Step 1:

In a blender, add peaches, then puree, until smooth. Set aside.

Step 2:

In a bowl, add warm water and gelatin, stir or whisk to mix, until dissolved. Set aside.

Step 3:

In a mixing bowl, add cream cheese and sugar, then using a hand mixer or stand mixer, medium speed, mix well, until light and fluffy.

Step 4:

Add vanilla extract and gelatin, then mix well.

Step 5:

Reduce to low speed, slowly add heavy cream, until mixed well and "soft peaks" form.

Checking for peaks:
Soft peaks are formed when you quickly dip the mixing beaters in and out once, pulling up some of the mixture into a peak but having it fall back down immediately into the rest of the mixture.

Step 6:
Add pureed peaches, then increase to medium speed, mix well, until thick and fluffy. Set aside.

Assembly Directions:
Step 1:
Retrieve crust, berries, and cream elements, then place on a work surface.

Step 2:
To crust, add 1 & 1/2 cups peach cream, then spread evenly.

Step 3:
Add all blackberries, spreading in an even layer. If sugar remains in berries bowl, then set aside.

Step 4:
Add remaining peach cream, then spread evenly.

Step 5:
Sprinkle to add set aside crumb mixture. If sugar leftover, then sprinkle to add sugar.

Step 6:
Cover with plastic wrap / film. Transfer to refrigerator to chill for at least 1 hour before serving.

Fresh Storage:
Cover with plastic wrap / film and store in the refrigerator. Use within 3 days.

Frozen Storage:
Do NOT freeze.

Your Notes:

_____

Round One Guess As to the Inspirational Movie:

_____

MOVIE FIFTEEN

Level One Hint:

- The inspired dish is made with a main element argued over by two of the sisters, who are like vinegar and oil, just before a baby is born.

Round Two Guess As to the Inspirational Movie:

MOVIE FIFTEEN

Level Two Hints:

- This 1997 comedic drama has roots is another food-centered movie, although the food changes from its Asian roots.

- This movie and its family Chef are grounded in cooking from the heart.

- At the end of the movie, the narrator tricks the family into gathering at Big Mama's house for one more dinner, where the 11-year old boy accidently sets fire to the kitchen.

- This family has been having a weekly, Sunday dinner for 40 years.

Round Three Guess As to the Inspirational Movie:

_____

MOVIE FIFTEEN

Level Three Hints:

- Cornbread served with Bacon & Shrimp & Creole Remoulade
- The inspirational movie begins with music, "A Song for Mama", and a wedding reception with dirty dancing that causes a scene.
- Big Mama always makes a traditional Mississippi-style Sunday dinner for her family in Chicago.
- This movie was made with an ensemble cast and was filmed in Chicago.
- Everyone is surprised to find out that the hidden money that was alluded to is real and was in the house all along, in Uncle Pete's television.
- In 2000, Showtime made a one-hour television series based upon the inspired movie.

Round Four Guess As to the Inspirational Movie:

MOVIE SIXTEEN

Course #1: Caprese Bites

Ingredients:
12 basil leaves (large), stemmed

12 cherry tomatoes

12 mozzarella, 1" cubes or balls

12 toothpicks

1 Tbsp extra virgin olive oil (quality makes a difference!)

1 Tbsp balsamic vinegar

salt, to taste

ground black pepper, to taste

Directions:
Step 1:

Lay down a basil leaf. To the middle, add a tomato and a mozzarella cube, then wrap the leaf so that ends overlap. To hold the wrapped leaf in place, insert a toothpick so through the leaf, through the tomato, through the mozzarella, and through the leaf on the other side. Set aside on a serving tray / platter.

Step 2:
Repeat Step 1 for all remaining 11 leaves.

Step 3:
Drizzle to add olive oil over all. Drizzle to add balsamic vinegar over all.

Step 4:
Sprinkle to add salt and pepper, to taste.

Step 5:
Cover with plastic wrap / film. Transfer to refrigerator until ready to serve.

Fresh Storage:
Cover with plastic wrap / film and store in the refrigerator. Use within 1 day.

Frozen Storage:
Do NOT freeze.

Your Notes:

_____

MOVIE SIXTEEN

Course #2: Sausage and Peppers served with Pasta

Ingredients:

3 Tbsp olive oil

1 Tbsp garlic, minced

1 yellow onion, cut into circle slices

1 red bell pepper, cored, seeded, and cut into slices

1 green bell pepper, cored, seeded, and cut into slices

1 orange bell pepper, cored, seeded, and cut into slices

6 fresh, sweet Italian sausages, cut 1" pieces

2 cups canned diced tomatoes, drained

1 cup dry red wine

1/4 tsp dried oregano

1/2 tsp dried basil

1/2 tsp salt

ground black pepper

4 servings dry pasta of your choice, serving portion
        according to pasta information on package /
        personal preference

Directions:

Step 1:

In a pan, on medium heat, add oil, onion, and sausage, then cook 5 minutes.

Step 2:

Add garlic, then cook 1 minute.

Step 3:

Add all the peppers, then cook 4 minutes.

Step 4:

Add tomatoes, wine, oregano, basil, and salt, then stir to mix well.

Step 5:

Reduce to medium-low heat. Simmer (almost boiling, but not at full boil) for 25 minutes.

Step 6:

During last 10 minutes of simmer, prepare pasta of choice according to directions for "al dente".

Step 7:
In a table serving bowl, add pasta and sausage with peppers mixture, then stir well to coat pasta with sauce.

Fresh Storage:
Cover with plastic wrap / film or place in a plastic sealable container and store in the refrigerator. Reheat in a pan. Use within 3 days.

Frozen Storage:
Do NOT freeze.

Your Notes:

_____

_____

MOVIE SIXTEEN

Course #3: Plum Grappa Granita

Ingredients:

2 cups plums, peeled and pitted

1/2 cup Moscato wine

2 pears, peeled and cored

2 Tbsp honey

6 Tbsp Grappa brandy

4 martini glasses

Directions:

Step 1:

In a food processor or blender, add plums, Moscato, pears, honey and Grappa, then blend, until smooth.

Step 2:

Transfer mixture to a 9x13" pan. Cover with plastic lid or plastic wrap / film.

Step 3:

Transfer covered pan to freezer for at least 3 hours, until frozen.

Step 4:
Remove frozen mixture and place on a work surface with
4 martini glasses.

Step 5:
With a spoon or ice cream scoop, drag and scrape
frozen mixture into curled shavings, then portion evenly
into martini glasses. Serve immediately.

Fresh Storage:
Do NOT fresh store.

Frozen Storage:
Cover dish with lid or plastic wrap / film and store in
freezer. May be frozen up to 4 weeks.

Your Notes:

_____

_____

Round One Guess As to the Inspirational Movie:

_____

MOVIE SIXTEEN

Level One Hint:

- The inspired dish was made by the character Clemenza, as he teaches another character how to cook the dish.

Round Two Guess As to the Inspirational Movie:

MOVIE SIXTEEN

Level Two Hints:

- Don't eat fish that has been delivered in a bulletproof vest.
- Clemenza is also responsible for another food moment when he says they should leave the gun but take the cannoli out of the car.
- It would have been difficult for the older male protagonist to eat during filming as he wore a dental appliance to alter the shape of his cheeks and jawline into a more "bulldog" looking face.

Round Three Guess As to the Inspirational Movie:

_____

MOVIE SIXTEEN

Level Three Hints:

- Sausage and Peppers served with Pasta
- Mario Puzo wrote both the novel and the screenplays for all of the movies in the trilogy; this inspirational movie was the first, released in 1972.
- Waking up next to a horse's head in your bed would make you consider your options.
- You'll make the younger male protagonist very angry if you insult his intelligence by claiming innocence, so just answer his questions and get in the car to leave for Vegas.

Round Four Guess As to the Inspirational Movie:

MOVIE SEVENTEEN

Course #1: Gallo Pinto

("Guy-O Pin-tow")

1/2 (2 cups) of the Basmati Rice: Frequently Used Side Item Recipes

Ingredients:
2 Tbsp vegetable oil
1/2 cup yellow onion, peeled and chopped
1 red OR orange bell pepper, seeded and chopped
2 tsp garlic, peeled, smashed, and minced
2 cups canned black beans (do not drain!)
5 Tbsp Salsa Lizano (Lizano Sauce)
salt, to taste
ground black pepper, to taste
4 Tbsp fresh cilantro, stemmed and chopped

Directions:

Step 1:

In a pan, on medium heat, add oil, onion, and pepper, then sauté, moving contents constantly, until onion is translucent.

Step 2:

Add garlic, then sauté 2 minutes.

Step 3:

Add un-drained beans, then bring to simmer (almost boiling, but not at full boil).

Step 4:

Add prepared rice, then stir to mix.

Step 5:

Add Salsa Lizano, then stir to mix.

Step 6:

Add salt and pepper, to taste.

Step 7:

Add cilantro, then stir to taste.

Step 8:

Serve with extra Salsa Lizano available for adding to personal taste.

Fresh Storage:

Cover with plastic wrap / film or place in a plastic sealable container and store in the refrigerator. Reheat in a pan. Use within 3 days.

Frozen Storage:

Do NOT freeze.

Your Notes:

_____

_____

MOVIE SEVENTEEN

Course #2: Puerco Pibil

Ingredients:

5 lbs pork butt

5 Tbsp whole annatto seeds

13 whole cloves

7 whole allspice

2 tsp cumin

1 Tbsp ground black pepper

2 Tbsp salt

2 jalapeño peppers, seeded and diced

1/2 cup oranges, juiced

1/2 cup white vinegar

3 Tbsp garlic, peeled, smashed, and minced

3 limes, juiced

3 lemons, juiced

3 oz "silver" tequila

Directions:

Step 1:
Cut pork butt into 1 – 2" pieces.

Step 2:
(Note: The annatto seeds will stain the grinder plastic parts and anything else it touches. These were used as one of the earliest clothing dyes for a red color, and these are still used to color many prepared foods today.) In a coffee or spice grinder, add annatto seeds, cloves, and allspice, then grind, until these are a very fine powder. You may need to do this in several small batches, as the annatto seeds are quite hard to grind.

Step 3:
Transfer ground spice mix powder to a non-staining bowl.

Step 4:
Add cumin, black pepper, and salt, then using a non-staining utensil, stir to mix well.

Step 5:
Add jalapeños, orange juice, vinegar, garlic, lime juice, lemon juice, and tequila, then using a non-staining utensil, stir to mix well.

Step 6:
Add pork pieces, then stir to coat pork with mixture.

Step 7:
Cover with plastic wrap / film, then transfer to refrigerator to marinate for a minimum of 4 hours, maximum of overnight.

Step 8:
Preheat oven to 300 degrees.

Step 9:
Transfer pork and marinade to a baking pan, then cover in heavy duty aluminum foil, "tenting" the foil so that it does not touch the pork.

Step 10:
Place the pan in the preheated oven, on the middle rack.
Bake for 4 - 5 hours, until pork falls apart when moved
with fork.

Fresh Storage:
Cover in a non-staining container with lid OR
plastic wrap / film and store in the refrigerator.
Reheat in a pan. Use within 5 days.

Frozen Storage:
Cover in a non-staining container with lid OR
plastic wrap / film, and store in freezer. Remove from
freezer and place in refrigerator to thaw before use.
Reheat in a pan. May be frozen up to 4 weeks.

Your Notes:

_____

_____

MOVIE SEVENTEEN

Course #3: Aztec Éclair Puffs

Éclair Puff Ingredients:

1/2 cup water

3 Tbsp butter

1 & 1/2 tsp sugar

1/8 tsp salt

1/2 cup & 2 Tbsp flour

3 eggs

1 gallon size "freezer" / heavy duty plastic sealable bag

parchment paper sheet to fit a baking sheet

1 toothpick

Éclair Puffs Directions:

Step 1:

Preheat oven to 425 degrees.

Step 2:

Line baking sheet with parchment paper sheet. Set aside.

Step 3:
In a pot, on medium high heat, add water, butter, sugar, and salt, then stir to mix well. Bring to boil.

Step 4:
Add flour, then stir to mix well. Reduce heat to medium-low heat.

Step 5:
Stir continuously, until the mix forms a ball and pulls away from the sides and bottom of the pot. Keep stirring for 3 minutes after the ball forms, then remove from heat.

Step 6:
Transfer dough ball to a mixing bowl, then either use a stand mixer with a paddle attachment *not regular beaters* (OR use a spatula and mix by hand), medium speed, paddle mix 1 minute.

Step 7:
Add 1 egg, then paddle mix until thoroughly mixed.

Step 8:
Repeat Step 7 for remaining 2 eggs.

Step 9:
Transfer dough into the gallon size heavy duty plastic sealable bag. Squeeze out excess air, then seal bag. Using kitchen scissors or a knife, cut a small notch piece out of a bottom corner.

Step 10:
Roll the empty part of the bag from the top, until the roll meets the dough. Hold the bag over the prepared baking sheet, then squeeze the dough into 2 dozen golf-ball-sized round ball shapes, keeping the tip of the bag into the dough forming, until it reaches the right size, then gently draw bag tip out of ball shape. Don't worry if these don't look great - these probably won't, as baking will fix the appearance.

Step 11:
Place baking sheet into the preheated oven, on the middle rack. Bake for 10 minutes.

Step 12:
Reduce oven to 350 degrees. Bake for 8 more minutes, until golden-brown colored.

Step 13:

Remove baking sheet from oven and place on a heat-safe surface, such as your stovetop.

Step 14:

Immediately, use a toothpick to poke a small hole in the top of each puff. Set aside to cool.

Aztec Filling Ingredients:

1 dried red chili pepper, seeded

1 tsp sugar

2 Tbsp cocoa powder

4 Tbsp confectioners' (powdered) sugar

1/8 tsp ground cinnamon

1 & 1/4 oz packet of unflavored gelatin

1/8 cup warm water (80 – 100 degrees)

1 cup dairy heavy whipping cream

1 gallon size "freezer" / heavy duty plastic sealable bag

Step 1:

In a food processor, spice grinder, or blender, add sugar and dried chili, then process until mixed well.

Step 2:
Transfer 1/8 tsp to a bowl. Place the remainder in a plastic sealable bag or container for future use.

Step 3:
Add cocoa powder, powdered sugar, and cinnamon, then stir to mix well. Set aside.

Step 4:
In a bowl, add warm water and gelatin, then stir or whisk to dissolve gelatin. Set aside.

Step 5:
In a mixing bowl, add cream, then using beaters with a stand or hand mixer, on high speed, beat until thickens.

Step 6:
Reduce to medium speed. Add gelatin and powder mix, then beat, until holds "stiff peaks".

Checking for peaks:
Stiff peaks are formed the same way but stay in the peak shape and do not fall down – like the topping of a meringue pie.

Step 7:

Transfer filling into the gallon size heavy duty plastic sealable bag. Squeeze out excess air, then seal bag. Using kitchen scissors or a knife, cut a very small notch piece out of a bottom corner.

Step 8:

Roll the empty part of the bag from the top, until the roll meets the filling. Set aside.

Step 9:

Some éclair puffs will have an opening already, but for those which do not, use the tip of a knife to make a small opening into the center of the puff's hollow air pocket, that can be accessed for filling.

Step 10:

Hold the bag up to the opening of an éclair puff, then squeeze cream filling from bag into puffball, until filled. Transfer filled éclair puff to a serving platter or storage container.

Step 11:

Repeat Step 10 for remaining 23 puffs.

Step 12:
Cover with lid or plastic wrap / film. Transfer to refrigerator to chill until ready to serve.

Fresh Storage:
Cover with plastic wrap / film or place in a plastic sealable bag or container and store in the refrigerator. Use within 1 days.

Frozen Storage:
Do NOT freeze.

Your Notes:

_____

_____

Round One Guess As to the Inspirational Movie:

_____

MOVIE SEVENTEEN

Level One Hint:

- The inspired dish is made by one Chef so well that Agent Sands kills him to restore balance to the world.

Round Two Guess As to the Inspirational Movie:

MOVIE SEVENTEEN

Level Two Hints:

- The male character of CIA Agent Sands eats the inspired dish in every restaurant he visits in the inspirational film.
- If you give yourself up to a retired agent, then make sure the agent buys your taco at the taco stand first.
- If you see a Clash of the Titans lunchbox, then check to see if $ 10,000 is being hidden inside of it.

Round Three Guess As to the Inspirational Movie:

MOVIE SEVENTEEN

Level Three Hints:

- Puerco Pibil

- The inspirational movie was written and directed by Robert Rodriguez and was the last in the "mariachi trilogy", released in 2003.

- Would you know the correct answer if you were asked if you are a Mexi-CAN or a Mexi-CAN'T?

- $10,000 is considered civilized by some but is also worth killing over for some.

- The guitar fighter offered to kill the cook, but Agent Sands did as it was convenient to where his car was parked.

Round Four Guess As to the Inspirational Movie:

_____

MOVIE EIGHTEEN

Course #1: Prosciutto Pears

Ingredients:
1/4 lb prosciutto sliced thinly
1 pear cored and cut 1" pieces
1/8 cup balsamic vinegar
toothpicks

Directions:
Step 1:
In a pan, medium-low heat, add balsamic vinegar, then cook, until it reaches the consistency of molasses.

Step 2:
Transfer into a bowl. Set aside.

Step 3:
Wrap a piece of pear in just enough prosciutto to cover it, then insert toothpick to hold together.

Step 4:

Dip wrapped pear in balsamic glaze. Place on a serving tray.

Step 5:

Repeat Step 3 & 4 for all remaining pieces of pear.

Fresh / Frozen Storage:

Do NOT store.

Your Notes:

_____

_____

MOVIE EIGHTEEN

Course #2: Mushroom Ravioli

Mushroom Ravioli Ingredients:

2 lb mushrooms, sliced

1 cup yellow onion, diced

4 Tbsp butter

1/4 tsp fresh thyme

1 Tbsp garlic, peeled, smashed, minced

1/2 cup dairy heavy whipping cream

1/2 cup white wine

3 cups asiago cheese, grated

1 tsp salt

1/2 tsp ground black pepper

1 & 1/2 cups all-purpose flour

1/4 cups semolina flour

3 eggs, beaten

2 eggs separated, yolks only kept

1/2 tsp olive oil

Mushroom Filling & Ravioli Directions:

Step 1:

In a pan, on medium heat, add butter and onion, then sauté, constantly stirring, until the onion begins to brown.

Step 2:

Add mushrooms, thyme and garlic, then cook, until mushrooms release liquid and begin to brown.

Step 3:

Add wine, cream, salt, and pepper, then simmer (almost boiling, but not at full boil), until the liquids are almost completely gone.

Step 4:

Remove from heat and transfer to a heat-safe surface, such as a cold burner.

Step 5:

Add cheese, then stir to mix well.

Step 6:

Transfer to a food processor, then puree. Set aside.

Step 7:

In a bowl, add 2 flours, eggs, yolks, and oil, then stir to mix dough well.

Step 8:

Knead dough for 3 minutes on floured work surface.

Step 9:

Cut dough into 3 equal portions.

Step 10:

Leave the dough on the work surface, then cover with plastic wrap / film. Set aside 30 minutes.

Step 11:

Roll out dough, then folding it over on top of itself.

Step 12:

Repeat Step 11 for 8 more times, until dough appears silky and is 1/8" thick.

Step 13:
Over 1 half-side of the pasta sheet, place 1 Tbsp mushroom mix, in a mound, 2" away from the corner edge.

Step 14:
Continue placing 1 Tbsp mounds of mushroom mix 2" apart, remembering to only place on 1 half-side of the pasta sheet.

Step 15:
Fold the empty half-side of the pasta sheet over, lining up the corners.

Step 16:
Using fingers, gently press to seal the top to the bottom around each of the 4 sides of each mound, making sure to not leave air pockets inside each square.

Step 17:
Cut out each square ravioli, then use a fork to gently crimp edges for a more secure seal. Set aside ravioli.

Step 18:
Repeat Step 17 for all remaining ravioli.

Sauce Ingredients:

2 Tbsp olive oil

1/4 cup yellow onion, diced 1/4"

1 Tbsp garlic, peeled, smashed, minced

1/4 tsp dried thyme

1/4 cup white wine

2 cups dairy heavy whipping cream

1 cup parmesan cheese, grated

salt, to taste

ground black pepper, to taste

2 Tbsp salt

Sauce Directions:

Step 1:

In a pan, on medium heat, add oil and onions, sauté 3 minutes.

Step 2:

Add garlic and thyme, sauté 1 minute.

Step 3:

Add white wine, then increase heat to medium-high.

Step 4:
Cook, until wine is reduce to only 25% of the original volume.

Step 5:
Add cream, then stir to mix well.

Step 6:
Reduce heat to simmer (almost boiling, but not at full boil), then simmer 3 minutes.

Step 7:
Add cheese, then stir to mix well. Reduce heat to low, then cook 3 minutes.

Step 8:
Add salt and pepper, to taste. Set aside.

Ravioli Assembly:
Step 1:
In a pot, on medium heat, add 4 quarts of water and add 2 Tbsp salt.

Step 2:
Bring water to simmer (almost boiling, but not at full boil), then cook ravioli for 3 minutes.

Step 3:
Remove ravioli, then transfer to a serving bowl.

Step 4:
Add sauce, then stir to mix well.

Fresh Storage:
Cover with plastic wrap / film and store in the refrigerator. Reheat in a pan. Use within 3 days.

Frozen Storage:
Cover dish with plastic wrap / film and store in freezer. Remove from freezer and place in refrigerator to thaw before use. Reheat in a pan. May be frozen up to 2 weeks.

Your Notes:

_____

_____

MOVIE EIGHTEEN

Course #3: Panna Cotta with

Fresh Berries

Ingredients:

3/4 cup whole (3%) dairy milk

1 & 1/4 oz packet of unflavored gelatin

2 & 1/2 cups dairy heavy whipping cream

3 Tbsp honey

1 Tbsp sugar

1/8 tsp salt

1 cup fresh berries: strawberry , raspberry ,blueberry

4 clear, colorless, glass dessert-sized bowls, goblets,
        martini glasses, or parfait glasses.

Directions:

Step 1:

In a pan, add milk and gelatin, then whisk to dissolve
gelatin. Set aside.

Step 2:

Turn heat to medium-low, then whisk to dissolve gelatin.

Step 3:
Add cream, honey, sugar, and salt, then stir until honey and sugar are completely dissolved into the mixture.

Step 4:
Transfer mixture into 4 clear, colorless, glasses.

Step 5:
Cover each glass piece with plastic wrap / film.

Step 6:
Transfer to a refrigerator, to chill for at least 4 hours.

Step 7:
Before serving, top each with a portion of fresh berries.

Fresh / Frozen Storage:
Do NOT store.

Your Notes:

_____

Round One Guess As to the Inspirational Movie:

MOVIE EIGHTEEN

Level One Hint:

- The inspired dish was ordered by the nervous female protagonist on a first date, however her date ordered nothing.

Round Two Guess As to the Inspirational Movie:

_____

MOVIE EIGHTEEN

Level Two Hints:

- The female protagonist's nickname is found in the restaurant's name from that first date.

- One of the male protagonists plays a type of hacky-sack with an apple, and he catches it in his hand in the same manner as seen in a popular snapshot shown for promotions for the movie.

- Be careful meeting people in a field, as you may be considered as a "snack" by some of them.

- If a family cooks an Italian meal for you in honor of having you over to their house, then do not refuse the meal, as a bowl will be broken.

Round Three Guess As to the Inspirational Movie:

MOVIE EIGHTEEN

Level Three Hints:

- Mushroom Ravioli

- The inspirational film was the first in a series, released in 2008, directed by Catherine Hardwicke, and based upon a novel.

- "Break a leg" can actually happen at a ballet studio of lessons past, but a cast can be a fashion statement at prom.

- You can go surfing at La Push Beach on the Quileute Reservation unless your family has an arrangement with The People of the tribe that says otherwise.

- Apotamkin aka The Cold One is a legend told by The People of the Quileute tribe.

- Port Angeles and Forks are real towns in Washington State.

Round Four Guess As to the Inspirational Movie:

MOVIE NINETEEN

Course #1: Grapefruit Salad

Ingredients:

2 large grapefruit (any color preference)

1 cup celery, diced 1/4"

2 Tbsp golden raisins

1/2 cup Honeycrisp apple, diced 1/2" (or similar
varietal)

4 tsp fresh mint, stemmed and chopped

1 cup romaine, torn into bite-sized pieces

2/3 cup plain yogurt (Greek, soy, or dairy)

1 Tbsp extra virgin olive oil

2 Tbsp oranges, peeled, seeded, and juiced

1/4 tsp salt

1/8 tsp ground white pepper

4 mint leaves, stemmed

4 clear, colorless, glass dessert-sized bowls, goblets,
martini glasses, or parfait glasses.

Directions:

Step 1:

Peel both grapefruit, removing pith (bitter, white underside of peel).

Step 2:

Cut membrane covering the outer edge of all segments.

Step 3:

Cut membranes in-between all segments, making sure to get V-shaped segments fully separated, then transfer all segments to a bowl.

Step 4:

Add celery, raisins, apple, mint, and romaine, then stir to mix well. Set aside.

Step 5:

In a bowl, add yogurt, olive oil, orange juice, salt, and white pepper, then whisk to mix well.

Step 6:

Add to grapefruit mixture, then stir to mix well.

Step 7:

Cover with plastic wrap / film. Transfer to a refrigerator for at least 30 minutes.

Step 8:

Portion into 4 clear, colorless, glass dessert-sized bowls, goblets, martini glasses, or parfait glasses.

Step 9:

Top with a mint leaf for garnish.

Fresh Storage:

Cover with plastic wrap / film and store in the refrigerator. Use within 1 days.

Frozen Storage:

Do NOT freeze.

Your Notes:

_____

_____

MOVIE NINETEEN

Course #2: Lamb Stew with Dried Plums

Ingredients:

4# leg of lamb, cubed 1"

1 Tbsp salt

2 tsp fresh rosemary, stemmed and chopped finely

2 tsp fresh thyme, stemmed and chopped finely

2 tsp fresh parsley, stemmed and chopped finely

1/2 cup flour

4 Tbsp vegetable oil

2 tsp garlic, peeled, smashed, and minced

18 pearl onions

1 cup celery, diced 1/4"

4 cups beef stock / broth

1 cup dried plums (prunes), halved

1 bay leaf

1 sprig rosemary

4 sprigs fresh thyme

2 cups carrots, diced 1/4"

3 cups potatoes, diced 1/2"

salt, to taste

ground black pepper, to taste

Directions:

Step 1:

On a cutting board, add lamb cubes, then trim any excessive fat.

Step 2:

Add salt. Set aside.

Step 3:

In a bowl, add rosemary, thyme, parsley, and flour, then stir to mix well.

Step 4:

Add lamb cubes, then stir to coat with flour mixture.

Step 5:

In a pot, on medium high heat, add oil and coated lamb cubes, then cook in a single layer, until lamb is browned. (May have to cook in multiple batches depending upon pot size.)

Step 6:

Remove browned lamb and transfer to a bowl. Set aside.

Step 7:
Add remaining flour mixture, onions, and celery, then stir to mix well and cook for 5 minutes.

Step 8:
Add browned lamb and garlic, then stir to mix well.

Step 9:
Add beef stock, then stir to mix well. Simmer for 5 minutes.

Step 10:
Add plums, then stir to mix well.

Step 11:
Gently place bay leaf, rosemary sprig, and thyme sprigs on top, then cover with lid. Simmer for 30 minutes.

Step 12:
Remove bay leaf and all sprigs, then set aside.

Step 13:
Add carrots and potatoes, then stir to mix well.

Step 14:
Gently place herbs on top again. Simmer for 1 hour.

Step 15:
Remove bay leaf and sprigs.

Fresh Storage:
Cover with plastic wrap / film or place in a plastic sealable container and store in the refrigerator. Reheat in a pan. Use within 3 days.

Frozen Storage:
Cover dish with plastic wrap / film or place in a plastic sealable container, and store in freezer. Remove from freezer and place in refrigerator to thaw before use. Reheat in a pan. May be frozen up to 4 weeks.

Your Notes:

_____

_____

MOVIE NINETEEN

Course #3: Cinnamon Mouse with Orange Segments

Ingredients:

2 tsp unflavored gelatin

2 Tbsp warm water (80-100 degrees)

1 cup whole (3%) dairy milk

1 tsp ground cinnamon

2 eggs separated, yolks only kept

3 Tbsp sugar

1/2 tsp vanilla extract

2/3 cup dairy heavy whipping cream

4 ceramic ramekins 6 oz each

1 orange, peeled, cored, seeded, and segmented

Directions:

Step 1:

In a bowl, add warm water and gelatin, then whisk to dissolve gelatin. Set aside.

Step 2:

In a pot, on medium heat, add milk and cinnamon, then whisk to mix well. Cook, until you see the first bubble, then reduce heat to medium-low.

Step 3:

In a bowl, add yolks and sugar, then whisk vigorously, until light and frothy.

Step 4:

While whisking yolks mixture vigorously, slowly drizzle the warm milk mix. (Adding the warm milk too fast will scramble your eggs!)

Step 5:

Transfer mixture from bowl back into the warm pot, on medium-low heat, then cook 12 minutes, until the mixture thickens enough so that when you dip a spoon in, the mixture coats the back of the spoon and does not drip off. You can double check by swiping a fingertip through the coated spoon and making sure that the line does not recover with mixture.

Step 6:
Remove pot from heat and place on a heat-safe surface, such as a cold burner.

Step 7:
Add gelatin mix and vanilla extract, then stir to mix well.

Step 8:
Transfer to a bowl, then cover with plastic wrap / film.

Step 9:
Transfer to refrigerator to chill for 1 hour, stirring occasionally.

Step 10:
In a mixing bowl, add cream. On high speed, using a hand or stand mixer, beat whipping cream to "stiff peaks". Set aside.

Checking for stiff peaks:
Stiff peaks are formed when you quickly dip the mixing beaters in and out once, pulling up some of the mixture into a peak, then it stays in the peak shape and does not fall down – like the topping of a meringue pie.

Step 11:
Retrieve chilled mixture from refrigerator, then gently fold into whipped cream, until mixed through.

Step 12:
Divide equally into 4 ramekins.

Step 13:
Cover each ramekin with plastic wrap / film. Transfer to refrigerator to chill at least 4 hours or up to 2 days.

Step 14:
Add warm tap water to a bowl. Set aside.

Step 15:
Insert a thin-blade knife along the inner edge of a ramekin. "Run" the knife all along the inner edge to separate the mousse from the ramekin edges.

Step 16:
Place all but the last 1/2" of a ramekin into the warm water for 5 seconds.

Step 17:
Invert the ramekin over a dessert plate, allowing the mousse to leave the ramekin.

Step 18:
Repeat Steps 15-17 for remaining 3 ramekins.

Step 19:
Lightly dust / sprinkle to add cinnamon, then top with equal portion of orange segments to each mousse.

Fresh Storage:
Cover with plastic wrap / film and store in the refrigerator. Use within 1 days.

Frozen Storage:
Do NOT freeze.

Your Notes:

_____

Round One Guess As to the Inspirational Movie:

_____

MOVIE NINETEEN

Level One Hint:

- The inspired dish is eaten by the female protagonist on the train to Panem and is her favorite Capitol dish.

Round Two Guess As to the Inspirational Movie:

MOVIE NINETEEN

Level Two Hints:

- Nightlock berries will kill a Foxface but will save you if you use these at a Cornucopia.
- With her father's archery set, the female protagonist supplemented her family's food rations.
- Shoot an apple out of a roasted pig's mouth and score 11 out of 12.

Round Three Guess As to the Inspirational Movie:

_____

MOVIE NINETEEN

Level Three Hints:

- Lamb Stew with Dried Plums
- Use a 3-finger salute to honor and say good-bye if you are from District 12.
- Use mockingjay calls and tracker jacker nests to defeat Careers.
- Caesar makes an engaging show host.

Round Four Guess As to the Inspirational Movie:

_____

MOVIE TWENTY

Course #1: Fried Green Tomatoes served with Dipping Sauce

Dipping Sauce Ingredients:

1 cup mayonnaise

3 Tbsp ketchup

2 Tbsp dill relish

1 & 1/2 tsp dry mustard

3 drops hot sauce

1/4 tsp salt

Dipping Sauce Directions:

Step 1:

In a bowl, add mayonnaise, ketchup, relish, mustard, hot sauce, and salt, then whisk to mix well.

Step 2:

Cover with plastic wrap / film.

Step 3:

Refrigerate until ready to use.

Fried Green Tomatoes Ingredients:

4 green tomatoes, cut into 1/4" rings

1 tsp salt

1/2 tsp ground black pepper

3/4 cup flour

1 Tbsp garlic powder

4 eggs

2 Tbsp whole (3%) dairy milk

1 & 1/2 cups "Panko" bread crumbs

1/8 tsp cayenne pepper

1/4 tsp paprika

vegetable oil

Fried Green Tomatoes Directions:

Step 1:

Transfer tomato slices to a wire rack, then add salt in even distribution over all slices. Set aside 30 minutes.

Step 2:

Pat tomato slices dry with paper towel.

Step 3:

Sprinkle to add pepper. Set aside.

Step 4:

In a bowl, add flour and garlic powder, then whisk to mix well. Set aside.

Step 5:

In another bowl, add eggs and milk, then whisk to mix well. Set aside.

Step 6:

In another bowl, add Panko, cayenne, and paprika, then whisk to mix well. Set aside.

Step 7:

To a pan, add vegetable oil, until 1" deep.

Step 8:

Using a thermometer (candy or digital), heat until 350 degrees.

Step 9:

Retrieve slices and 3 bowl mixtures.

Step 10:
Take 1 tomato slice. Drag it back and forth on both sides in the flour mixture bowl. Shake off excess flour back into bowl.

Step 11:
Drag coated slice back and forth on both sides in egg mixture bowl, coating thoroughly.

Step 12:
Drag wet slice back and forth on both sides in Panko mixture bowl, coating thoroughly. Set aside.

Step 13:
Repeat Steps 10 – 12 for remaining tomato slices.

Step 14:
Line a plate with 5 layers of paper towels. Set aside.

Step 15:
Into the hot oil pan, gently place a few tomato slices, in a single layer. Do not allow the temperature to drop more than 10 degrees, so if at that drop maximum, stop adding slices, even if room allows for these.

Step 16:
Cook 2 minutes, until golden-brown colored.

Step 17:
Flip slices, then cook another 2 minutes, until golden-brown colored.

Step 18:
Remove slices, then transfer to paper towel covered plate, to drain.

Step 19:
Serve with dipping sauce.

Fresh Storage:
Cover with plastic wrap / film or place in a plastic sealable bag and store in the refrigerator. Reheat in a pan. Use within 1 days.

Frozen Storage:
Do NOT freeze.

Your Notes:

_____

MOVIE TWENTY

Course #2: Pork Chops served with Greens in a Cherries & Port Wine Reduction

Ingredients:

4 pork 6oz chops

1 tsp salt

1/2 ground black pepper

2 Tbsp olive oil

1/4 cup yellow onions, diced 1/4"

1/2 cup black sweet cherries (frozen or fresh)

1/2 cup chicken stock / broth

1/2 cup "ruby" port wine (not tawny!)

6 cups fresh greens, varietal of choice

Directions:

Step 1:

To a plate, add pork chops.

Step 2:

Sprinkle to add salt and pepper. Set aside.

Step 3:

In a pan, on medium heat, add oil and pork chops, then cook, until golden-brown color appears on underneath side.

Step 4:

Flip pork, then brown other side.

Step 5:

Transfer chops to a plate. Set aside.

Step 6:

To the hot pan, on medium heat, add onion, then cook, stirring occasionally, until begin to brown.

Step 7:

Add chicken stock, cherries, and port wine, then stir to mix well.

Step 8:

Bring to a simmer (almost boiling, but not at full boil).

Step 9:

Simmer, until only 30% of original volume is left in the pan.

Step 10:

Add pork chops, then stir well.

Step 11:

Drop in greens, then cook 5 minutes, until greens are wilted and tender.

Step 12:

Serve pork chops on top of greens and garnish with cherries and sauce.

Fresh Storage:

Cover with plastic wrap / film or place in a plastic sealable bag and store in the refrigerator. Reheat in a pan. Use within 3 days.

Frozen Storage:

Cover dish with plastic wrap / film or place in a plastic sealable bag, and store in freezer. Remove from freezer and place in refrigerator to thaw before use. Reheat in a pan. May be frozen up to 2 weeks.

Your Notes:

_____

_____

MOVIE TWENTY

Course #3: Bourbon Pecan Tart

Tart Crust Ingredients:

1 & 1/8 cups flour

1/8 cup sugar

1/8 tsp salt

1/2 cup butter, cut 1/4" or smaller pieces

1/8 cup (or more) ice water

10" tart pan with a removable bottom plate

2 cups of either dry rice or dry beans – any kind

Tart Crust Directions:

Step 1:

In a bowl, add flour, sugar, and salt, then with bare hands, stir to mix well.

Step 2:

Add butter, then with bare hands in the mixture, place your thumbs on your littlest fingers, then slide your thumbs across the fingertips of all your other fingers, then repeat that motion, to break up the butter and mix it with the flour at the same time, until there are no butter pieces left larger than a small pea. Dough will be crumbly.

Step 3:

Add water, then using bare hands, mix thoroughly, until dough becomes sticky and can form a round ball shape that does not crumble apart.

Note: Depending upon humidity and temperature, you may need to add a little more or less water to get dough to this consistency. If dough is not absorbing all the water, then add a little bit of flour at a time and mix it in, until the excess water is absorbed into the dough.

Step 4:

Using bare hands, shape dough into a round ball shape,

Step 5:

Place ball in bowl, cover bowl with plastic wrap / film.

Step 6:
Transfer to refrigerator, to chill for 30 minutes.

Step 7:
Sprinkle flour on a flat, clean, dry work surface. Set aside.

Step 8:
Retrieve dough bowl from refrigerator, then place dough ball on floured surface.

Step 9:
On the floured work surface, using a rolling pin, press down and roll out from the center of the dough ball, over and over, each time rolling in a different direction, until you roll out a 12" circle of even thickness.

Step 10:
Once rolled out to the right size, you can fix any little tears by wetting your finger with ice water and press the dough to "seam" the rip closed. If needed, then use a little "patch" of dough to close the tear, "seaming" the patch with your wet fingers.

Step 11:
Gently lift one edge of your dough to fold the dough circle in half.

Step 12:
Carefully move the entire circle of dough onto your tart pan, adjusting to cover one half and having some overlapping the pan edge, then unfold the circle to cover the entire pan and have some dough overlapping all of the pan edges.

Step 13:
Gently press the dough so that it lies against the insides of the pan.

Step 14:
Run a knife along the outer edge of the pie plate to trim off the excess dough.

Step 15:
Transfer tart pan to refrigerator, to chill 30 minutes.

Step 16:
Preheat oven to 375 degrees.

Step 17:
Remove tart pan and place on a work surface. Gently place 1 piece of aluminum foil on the bottom of the pan, covering the dough.

Step 18:
Add 2 cups of either dry rice or dry beans, spreading until these are in a single layer on the foil. These will hold down the foil and thus the crust, not allowing the crust to expand too much during baking.

Step 19:
Place the tart pan in the preheated oven, on the middle rack. Bake for 20 minutes.

Step 20:
Remove beans / rice and foil. Bake another 10 minutes, until light golden-brown colored.

(*Storage for beans / rice)

Step 21:

Remove tart pan from oven, and place on a heat-safe surface, such as your stovetop.

Step 22:

Set aside to cool.

Tart Filling Ingredients:

3 eggs

1/2 cup brown sugar

3/4 cup Golden syrup (found in stores near molasses)

4 Tbsp butter, melted

2 Tbsp bourbon

1 tsp vanilla extract

1/4 tsp salt

2 cups pecan halves

Tart Filling Directions:

Step 1:

In a mixing bowl, add eggs and sugar, using a hand or stand mixer, medium speed, beat well.

Step 2:

Add golden syrup, butter, bourbon, vanilla extract, and salt, then beat, until well blended.

Step 3:

Add pecans, then stir with a spatula.

Step 4:

Pour filling into prepared crust.

Step 5:

Place tart pan in preheated oven, on the middle rack. Bake for 25 minutes, until center is not soupy or jiggly.

Step 6:

Remove tart pan from oven, then place on a wire rack to cool for at least 45 minutes.

Fresh Storage:

Cover with plastic wrap / film and store in the refrigerator. Use within 5 days.

Frozen Storage:

Cover with plastic wrap / film and store in freezer. Remove from freezer and place in refrigerator to thaw before use. May be frozen up to 4 weeks.

Storage for Dried Beans / Rice:

You can use these multiple times and with baking crusts of different types, so store these in a sealable plastic bag or container out of direct sunlight or heat, such as a pantry or dry goods cupboard.

Your Notes:

_____

Round One Guess As to the Inspirational Movie:

_____

MOVIE TWENTY

Level One Hint:

- The inspired dish is served at the Whistle Stop Café in Alabama.

Round Two Guess As to the Inspirational Movie:

MOVIE TWENTY

Level Two Hints:

- Whistle Stop Café was based upon the Irondale Café in Irondale, Alabama and is the setting in the novel by Fannie Flagg that the inspirational movie was based upon.

- A food fight scene was shown to symbolize love-making between two female protagonists, and while most of the novel's lesbian content was removed for the movie, the film still earned the GLADD Media Award for best lesbian content.

- Sipsey, a cook, killed Frank with a cast iron skillet.

- Patti LaBelle sang Barbeque Bess for the soundtrack of the inspired film.

Round Three Guess As to the Inspirational Movie:

MOVIE TWENTY

Level Three Hints:

- Fried Green Tomatoes served with Dipping Sauce
- Older people with better insurance have the advantage over younger people who are fast.
- One of the female protagonists is nicknamed The Bee Charmer.
- A flock of ducks was accused for the loss of a lake in the area.

Round Four Guess As to the Inspirational Movie:

_____

MOVIE TWENTY-ONE

Course #1: Hoppin John

Creole Seasoning Ingredients:
* You may also buy a premade Creole seasoning and skip this recipe section.

5 Tbsp sweet paprika

4 Tbsp salt

2 Tbsp onion powder

2 Tbsp garlic powder

2 Tbsp dried oregano leaves

2 Tbsp dried basil

1 Tbsp dried thyme leaves

1 Tbsp ground black pepper

1 Tbsp ground white pepper

1 Tbsp cayenne pepper

1 Tbsp celery seed

Creole Seasoning Directions:

Step 1:

In a food processor/spice grinder, add paprika, salt, onion powder, garlic powder, oregano, basil, thyme, ground black pepper, ground white pepper, cayenne pepper, and celery seed, then process for 5 seconds.

Step 2:

Transfer to covered container or plastic sealable bag. Set aside.

Hoppin John Ingredients:

1 & 1/2 cups long-grain white rice

1/3 # thick-cut bacon, diced 1/4"

1 cup yellow onion, diced 1/4"

1 stalk / rib celery, diced 1/4"

1 tsp garlic, peeled, smashed, and minced

32 oz canned black-eyed peas, drained and rinsed

1 cup chicken stock / broth

1 bay leaf

1 tsp thyme, stemmed

1 tsp Creole seasoning (recipe or premade)

2 green onions, sliced thinly

Lisa Shipley and James Shipley

Hoppin John Directions:

Step 1:

Cook rice according to package directions. Set aside.

Step 2:

In a pan, on medium heat, add bacon, then cook 3 minutes.

Step 3:

Flip bacon over, then cook 3 minutes.

Step 4:

Place finished bacon aside.

Step 5:

From the used bacon pan, drain out all but 2 Tbsp of bacon grease.

Step 6:

Add onion and celery, then stir. Cook for 3 minutes.

Step 7:

Add garlic, then stir. Cook for 1 minute.

426

Step 8:
Add black-eyed peas, chicken stock, bay leaf, thyme, and Creole seasoning, then stir to mix well. Cook 20 minutes, until peas are soft.

Step 9:
Add cooked rice, then stir to mix well.

Step 10:
Sprinkle to add green onion.

Fresh Storage:
Cover with plastic wrap / film or place in a plastic sealable container and store in the refrigerator. Reheat in a pan. Use within 3 days.

Frozen Storage:
Cover dish with plastic wrap / film or place in a plastic sealable container, and store in freezer. Remove from freezer and place in refrigerator to thaw before use. Reheat in a pan. May be frozen up to 2 weeks.

Your Notes:

___

MOVIE TWENTY-ONE

Course #2: Shrimp Sunset Sauté served with Angel Hair Pasta

Ingredients:

3 Tbsp olive oil

1/4 cup yellow onion, diced 1/4"

1 red pepper, seeded and diced 1/4"

2 tsp garlic, peeled, smashed, and minced

1 lb medium shrimp, removed tail, deveined, and shelled

1/2 tsp salt

1/4 tsp ground black pepper

1 Roma tomato, diced 1/4"

1/4 cup chicken stock / broth

1/4 cup dairy heavy whipping cream

1/3 cup Parmesan cheese, shredded

8 oz angel hair pasta

Directions:

Step 1:

In a pan, on medium heat, add oil, onion, and red pepper, then stir. Cook for 3 minutes, stirring occasionally.

Step 2:
Add garlic, shrimp, salt, and pepper, then stir to mix well.
Cook, stirring occasionally, until shrimp turns red on
both sides.

Step 3:
Add diced tomato, chicken stock, cream, and cheese,
then stir to mix well.

Step 4:
Increase to medium-high heat, then bring to simmer
(almost boiling but not at full boil). Stir again, then
remove from heat and place on a heat-safe surface, such
as a cold burner. Set aside.

Step 5:
Cook pasta according to directions on package for "al
dente".

Step 6:
To serve: Either add pasta then add shrimp mixture
OR add pasta to shrimp mixture and stir to mix well.

Fresh Storage:

Cover with plastic wrap / film and store in the refrigerator. Reheat in a pan. Use within 1 day.

Frozen Storage:

Do NOT freeze.

Your Notes:

_____

_____

MOVIE TWENTY-ONE

Course #3: Beignets

Ingredients:

1 cup warm water (80 – 100 degrees)

1/4 cup sugar

1 packet active dry yeast

1 egg, room temperature and beaten

2 Tbsp butter, softened at room temperature

1/2 cup evaporated milk

4 cups flour

1/2 tsp salt

vegetable oil - for deep frying

1 cup powdered sugar

Directions:

Step 1:

Spray a bowl with non-stick vegetable oil cooking spray. Set aside.

Step 2:

In a mixing bowl, add water, sugar, and yeast in bowl, then stir. Set aside 2 minutes.

Step 3:

Add egg, butter, milk, flour, and salt, then using a hand or stand mixer, beat, low speed, until smooth.

Step 4:

Transfer dough to prepared bowl, then cover with plastic wrap / film.

Step 5:

Transfer to refrigerator, to chill at least 3 hours, or overnight. (At this point only, the dough can be stored for up to 1 week in the refrigerator and can be stored in the freezer for up to 1 month.)

Step 6:

Sprinkle flour onto a flat, clean, dry work surface.

Step 7:
On the floured work surface, using a rolling pin, press down and roll out from the center of the dough ball, over and over, each time rolling in a different direction, until you roll out a 1/2" square of even thickness about 18" across.

Step 8:
Cut the dough into 3" squares. Set aside.

Step 9:
Put a serving plate / platter near the stovetop area, then place 5 pieces of paper towel on top of the plate. Set aside.

Step 10:
In a deep pot, bring 3" of oil to 350 degrees. Check and maintain heat, using a candy thermometer.

Step 11:
Gently place 3 dough pieces side by side in the oil, then fry 2 minutes.

Step 12:
Turn over dough pieces, then fry 1-2 minutes, until puff up and turn golden-brown colored.

Step 13:
Remove beignets and transfer to prepared plate with paper towels.

Step 14:
Sprinkle to add powdered sugar. Serve immediately.

Step 15:
Repeat Steps 11 – 14, until all remaining dough has been made into beignets.

Fresh / Frozen Storage:
Do NOT store.

Your Notes:

_____

Round One Guess As to the Inspirational Movie:

_____

MOVIE TWENTY-ONE

Level One Hint:

- The inspired dish is based upon a scene in the inspirational movie where two buddies in the Vietnam Conflict discuss the key ingredient.

Round Two Guess As to the Inspirational Movie:

MOVIE TWENTY-ONE

Level Two Hints:

- One of the key characters knew that this key ingredient in the inspired dish is one of common "sea fruits" or "fruits of the sea", known as Fruits De Mer in France and Fruitti Di Mare in Italy.
- The Doors' song "Soul Kitchen" is used in one of the Vietnam Conflict scenes in the inspirational movie.
- The themed emporium from the inspirational film has been used to theme real restaurants in 7 countries, including the United States of America.
- The male protagonist enjoyed free food and Dr. Pepper sodas while he visited with the President.

Round Three Guess As to the Inspirational Movie:

MOVIE TWENTY-ONE

Level Three Hints:

- Shrimp Sunset Sauté served with Angel Hair Pasta
- A park bench is the setting for many memorable quotes, including several about what the male protagonist's mother taught him.
- The male protagonist's real-life, younger brother stunt-doubled him in many of the running sequences.
- This 1994 inspirational epic film was based upon a 1986 novel by Winston Groom.

Round Four Guess As to the Inspirational Movie:

MOVIE TWENTY-TWO

Course #1: Duck Hash served on Toasted Baguette Bread

Baguette Bread: Frequently Used Side Item Recipes

Ingredients:

1 whole 5lb duck (should be 2 - 3 lbs of meat)

2 Tbsp salt

1/2 bay leaf

1 1/2 tsp fresh thyme

2 tsp fresh parsley

1/4 tsp ground black pepper

1 tsp garlic, peeled, smashed, and minced

2 Tbsp duck fat

1/2 cup potato, 1/8" diced

1 & 1/2 cups duck confit meat

1/2 cup onion, diced 1/8"

1/2 tsp salt

1/8 tsp ground black pepper

4 eggs

1 baguette recipe

1 Tbsp olive oil

Directions:

Step 1:

Remove as much of the skin and fat from the whole duck as possible. Set aside duck separately from skin and fat.

Step 2:

In a pot, on low heat, add 1 Tbsp tap water, duck skin, and duck fat. Cover with a lid, then cook 2 hours to render fat. Set aside.

Step 3:

In a blender or food processor, add salt, bay leaf, thyme, parsley, pepper, and garlic, then "pulse" speed, until mixed well. Set aside.

Step 4:

Preheat oven to 190 degrees.

Step 5:

Remove meat from duck breasts, then transfer meat to an oven-safe pot or pan, with an oven-safe lid.

Step 6:
Remove legs. Add to pot / pan with breast meat.

Step 7:
Pick over duck carefully to ensure that no fat or meat remains. Add any pieces to the oven-safe pot or pan.

Step 8:
Add rendered fat to meat.

Step 9:
Place pot / pan, covered, in the preheated oven, on the middle rack. Bake 8 hours, covered.

Step 10:
Transfer pot / pan to a heat-safe surface, such as your stovetop.

Step 11:
Pick off all meat from legs and discard any bones.

Step 12:
Separate meat and fat into different bowls.

Step 13:

If storing until the day of the dinner, then cover bowls with plastic wrap / film, and transfer to refrigerator, until ready to use, up to 5 days.

OR

If using immediately, then set aside bowls.

Step 14:

Retrieve baguette bread made from Frequently Used Side Item Recipes.

Step 15:

With a serrated / bread knife, cut slices 1/2+" thick.

Step 16:

Using a pastry brush, brush olive oil onto bread slices.

Step 17:

Using broiler feature of oven OR a grill top, high heat, toast bread slices, until golden-brown colored on top.

Step 18:

Flip bread slices, then broil / grill until golden-brown colored on top.

Step 19:

Remove bread slices and transfer to a clean, dry work surface or serving platter. Set aside.

Step 20:

In a pan, on medium heat, add 2 Tbsp saved duck fat and potato, then stir to mix well. Cook, until potato begins to get crispy.

Step 21:

Add onion, then stir to mix well. Cook for 2 minutes.

Step 22:

Add duck, salt and pepper, then stir to mix well. Cook, until everything is heated through, stirring occasionally. While heating through, do Step 23.

Step 23:

In a pot, on medium-high heat, bring 3 quarts of water to boil, then reduce heat to simmer (almost boiling, but not fully boiling).

Step 24:

Add carefully crack eggs by gently slip these into the water, then cook 2 minutes, until beginning to get firm.

Step 25:

With slotted spoon, remove eggs carefully and set aside.

Step 26:

For each person, portion 4 toasted slices of baguette, an equal amount of duck hash, and 1 poached egg on top. Offer hot sauce as an optional condiment.

Fresh / Frozen Storage:

Once assembled, do NOT store.

Frozen Storage:

Excess duck fat rendered can be placed separately in a plastic sealable container with a lid, then place in freezer and store for up to 3 months. Can be used for multiple other dishes as a replacement for oil for extra flavor.

Your Notes:

_____

MOVIE TWENTY-TWO

Course #2: Sea Scallops served with Asparagus & Tangerine Sauce

Ingredients:

1 lb asparagus

2 Tbsp olive oil

1/2 tsp salt

2 Tbsp olive oil

2 lb large sea scallops

1/2 tsp ground black pepper

3/4 tsp salt

3/4 cup dry white vermouth

3/4 cup fresh tangerine juice

2 Tbsp shallot, chopped finely

1/4 cup butter

Directions:

Step 1:

Cut asparagus to remove woody end. Set aside stalks.

Step 2:

Cut remaining stalks into 2" pieces.

Step 3:

In a pan, on medium heat, add oil, asparagus, and salt, then stir to mix. Cook 5 minutes, until vibrant green and beginning to soften.

Step 4:

Remove asparagus from pan and set aside. Wipe out pan and set aside to use for Step 8.

Step 5:

With a folded paper towel, blot to dry scallop. Place dry scallop in a bowl, set aside.

Step 6:

Repeat Step 5 for all remaining scallops.

Step 7:

Sprinkle to add salt and pepper, turning scallops to evenly coat with seasonings. Set aside.

Step 8:

In a pan, on medium heat, add oil and scallops. Cook thawed and dried scallops 2-3 minutes, until golden-brown colored on bottom side.

Step 9:

Flip scallops, then cook another 2-3 minutes, until golden-brown on bottom side.

Step 10:

Remove scallops to a clean bowl, then set aside.

Step 11:

To same pan, on medium heat, add shallots, then sauté for 2 minutes, until translucent.

Step 12:

Add vermouth and juice, then stir to mix well. Cook, until liquid reduced to 1/2 cup volume.

Step 13:
Add butter, then whisk to mix well.

Step 14:
Add scallops, then stir to mix well. Cook 1 minute.

Step 15:
Add asparagus, then stir to mix well. Cook 1 minute.

Step 16:
Transfer scallops to serving plates, then add asparagus and tangerine sauce to serving plates.

Fresh / Frozen Storage:
Do NOT store.

Your Notes:

_____

_____

MOVIE TWENTY-TWO

Course #3: Crème Brûlée with Orange

Ingredients:

1/4 cup orange marmalade

2 cups dairy heavy whipping cream

2 tsp vanilla extract

6 eggs, separated, yolks only kept

1/3 cup sugar

8 tsp sugar

4 ceramic 6 oz ramekins

hand-held blowtorch / blow lamp – buy at a hardware
    store and keep only for food use, never use a
    torch on food that has been used on non-food
    items

Directions:

Step 1:

Preheat the oven to 325 degrees.

Step 2:

Place an equal amount of marmalade into each ramekin.
Set aside.

Step 3:

In a pot, on medium high heat, add cream and bring to simmer (almost boiling, but not at full boil).

Step 4:

Transfer pot to a heat-safe surface, such as a cold burner.

Step 5:

Add vanilla extract, then stir to mix well. Set aside.

Step 6:

In a bowl, add eggs yolks and sugar, then whisk, until color lightens.

Step 7:

Continue to whisk yolks, and slowly drizzle in warm cream mixture. Adding cream too fast will scramble the eggs!

Step 8:

Strain the mix through a fine mesh strainer and in equal parts into prepared ramekins.

Step 9:

Transfer 4 ramekins into a baking pan with space left around each. Add water into the baking pan until comes up 2" on the outer side of the ramekins. This creates a "water bath" for the custard.

Step 10:

Place the double-pan set into the preheated oven, on the middle rack. Bake for 45 minutes, until custard looking like pudding but center moves slightly when ramekin is jiggled.

Step 11:

Remove double-pan set from oven and place on a heat-safe surface, such as a cold stovetop. Carefully remove the inner pan from its "water bath" and place it on a wire rack that has a dish-towel covering it. Set aside for 30 minutes.

Step 12:

Cover ramekins with plastic wrap / film, then place in refrigerator to chill, until ready to serve.

Step 13:
15 minutes before serving, transfer ramekins to a work surface.

Step 14:
For 1 ramekin, sprinkle to add 1 tsp of sugar on top.

Step 15:
Using a hand-held food-only blowtorch, touch the blue flame only to the sugar, sweeping back and forth, melting the sugar into a golden-brown colored, crisp caramel. Be quick with the melting process as too much exposure to the blowtorch will make the custard runny.

Step 16:
Set ramekin aside for 2 minutes to cool off.

Step 17:
Repeat Steps 15 & 16 for all remaining ramekins of custard.

Step 18:

Repeat Steps 14 – 17 for second crispy layer.

Fresh Storage:

For ramekins at Step 12 stage, cover with plastic wrap / film and store in the refrigerator. Use within 3 days. **Do not store past Step 12.**

Frozen Storage:

Do NOT freeze.

Your Notes:

_____

_____

Round One Guess As to the Inspirational Movie:

_____

MOVIE TWENTY-TWO

Level One Hint:

- The inspired dish is made by the female protagonist while she is doing a cooking demonstration at work in the cookware area.

Round Two Guess As to the Inspirational Movie:

MOVIE TWENTY-TWO

Level Two Hints:

- The female protagonist makes a famous Chef very happy as she orders all of the specials and wants no substitutions.
- The female protagonist and the famous Chef know the secret to life... butter.
- The female protagonist enjoys following along with Emeril's television cooking show, cooking wonderful meals that she doesn't eat but does photograph.
- If you are too shy around an attractive co-worker, then just buy a grill from him.

Round Three Guess As to the Inspirational Movie:

_____

MOVIE TWENTY-TWO

Level Three Hints:

- Duck Hash served on Toasted Baguette Bread
- The Book of Possibilities becomes a guide to the female protagonist as she decides to drastically change away from her shy, money-saving, self-denying lifestyle.
- The female protagonist arrives at The Czech Republic's The Grand Hotel Pupp with helicopter fanfare and is discussed by hotel staff by her previous employer, Matthew Kragen, and by his lover / secretary.
- Chef Didier never cooks the same specials two days in a row.
- Georgia gets the opportunity to cook with Chef Didier at his restaurant and at hers.

Round Four Guess As to the Inspirational Movie:

MOVIE TWENTY-THREE

Course #1: Pepperoncini Bites

Ingredients:

6 Tbsp cream cheese
1 Tbsp chives, minced
16 whole pepperoncini, tops removed
16 slices salami, 3" across

Directions:

Step 1:
In a mixing bowl, add cream cheese and chives, then using hand or stand mixer, beat on medium speed, until light and fluffy.

Step 2:
Transfer filling into a quart/sandwich-size heavy duty plastic sealable bag.

Step 3:
Squeeze out excess air, then seal bag.

Step 4:

Using kitchen scissors or a knife, cut a very small notch piece out of a bottom corner.

Step 5:

Roll the empty part of the bag from the top, until the roll meets the filling. Set aside.

Step 6:

With bare hands, place a finger in the middle of a salami slice, insert slice into a pepperoncini, so that the salami becomes a lining, leaving a space in the middle of the pepper.

Step 7:

Hold the bag up to the opening of the pepperoncini, then squeeze cream filling from bag into pepper, until filled. Set aside.

Step 8:

Repeat Steps 6 & 7, until all pepperoncini are filled.

Fresh Storage:

Cover with plastic wrap / film or place in a plastic sealable bag or container and store in the refrigerator. Use within 2 days.

Frozen Storage:

Do NOT freeze.

Your Notes:

_____

_____

MOVIE TWENTY-THREE

Course #2: Chicken Salad with Goat Cheese served with Balsamic Vinaigrette Dressing

Ingredients:

2 skinless, boneless 6 oz chicken breasts

1/2 tsp salt

1/8 tsp ground black pepper

1/2 tsp garlic, minced

1/4 cup balsamic vinegar

1 Tbsp Dijon mustard

3/4 cup extra virgin olive oil

salt, to taste

ground black pepper, to taste

8 cups mesclun greens

1 cup dried cranberries

1/2 cup toasted pecans - halved

1 Tbsp fresh thyme, stemmed and chopped finely

4 oz goat cheese

Directions:

Step 1:

Preheat oven to 400 degrees.

Step 2:

In a baking pan, add chicken. Sprinkle to add salt and pepper evenly on both sides.

Step 3:

Place pan in preheated oven, on the middle rack. Bake for 20 - 25 minutes, until internal temperature reaches 180 degrees on your thermometer.

Step 4:

Remove pan from oven and set aside on a heat-safe surface, such as your stovetop. Set aside.

Step 5:

In a bowl, add garlic and using the back-side of a spoon against the side of the bowl (or in a mortar and pestle), grind it into a paste.

Step 6:

Add vinegar and mustard, then whisk to mix well.

Step 7:
While whisking vigorously and continuously, slowly drizzle in oil to form an emulsion.

Step 8:
Add salt and pepper, to taste, then whisk to mix well. Set aside.

Step 9:
In a bowl, add mesclun, cranberries, pecans, and thyme, then stir to mix well.

Step 10:
Add 1/2 of dressing, then toss to mix well.

Step 11:
Portion equal amounts onto serving plates.

Step 12:
Place chicken on a cutting board, then cut slices of chicken 1/4" thick, against the grain of the meat.

Step 13:
Add chicken in equal amounts to the plated salad mixes.

Step 14:
Add goat cheese in equal amounts to the plated salad mixes.

Step 15:
Serve remaining dressing with salads for adding according to individual preference.

Fresh Storage:
Cover remaining dressing with plastic wrap / film or place in a sealable container and store in the refrigerator. Use within 5 days. Shake or whisk well before reuse.

Do not store assembled salads.

Frozen Storage:
Do NOT freeze.

Your Notes:

_____

_____

MOVIE TWENTY-THREE

Course #3: Tiramisu

Ingredients:

5 eggs, separated, kept yolks and whites, separate bowls

1 tsp vanilla extract

1 & 1/2 Tbsp sugar

7/8 cup flour

1 & 1/2 Tbsp sugar

1 cup mascarpone

1 tsp vanilla extract

3 Tbsp Tia Maria

2/3 cup prepared strong coffee or espresso, chilled

3/4 cup dairy heavy whipping cream

5 Tbsp confectioner's (powdered) sugar

4 martini glasses

1 bar of dark chocolate (70 - 80%)

1 tsp cocoa powder

Directions:

Step 1:
Preheat oven to 350 degrees.

Step 2:
Place parchment paper on a baking sheet / tray. Set aside.

Step 3:
In a mixing bowl, add egg yolks, then using a hand or stand mixer, medium speed, beat, until pale yellow colored.

Step 4:
Add sugar and vanilla extract, then beat to mix well.

Step 5:
Beat, medium speed, until yolks increase in volume and form a ribbon, which takes 5 seconds to fade when you turn off the mixer.

Step 6:
Remove beaters from mixing bowl. Transfer yolk mix to a bowl, taking care not to deflate the yolk mix.

Step 7:
Add flour, then gently fold, taking care not to deflate the yolk mix. Set aside.

Step 8:
In a clean, dry mixing bowl, add egg whites, then with hand or stand mixer, medium speed, beat, until frothy.

Step 9:
Add sugar, then beat, until forms stiff peaks.

Checking for stiff peaks:
Stiff peaks are formed when you quickly dip the mixing beaters in and out once, pulling up some of the mixture into a peak, then it stays in the peak shape and does not fall down – like the topping of a meringue pie.

Step 10:
Add 1/3 of egg white mixture into the egg yolk mixture, then gently fold, taking care not to deflate either mix.

Step 11:
Repeat Step 10 for remaining mixture.

Step 12:
With a spatula, spread batter gently over prepared baking sheet, until 1" even thickness.

Step 13:
Place sheet in the preheated oven, on the middle rack. Bake for 15 minutes.

Step 14:
Sponge should be golden-colored, dry, and springy when you touch it. If not, then bake longer.

Step 15:
Remove from oven and place on a wire rack to cool. Set aside.

(Chef note: I like to make this sheet of ladyfingers rather than individual fingers. The important thing is to make them fresh. Nothing ruins a Tiramisu like stale biscuits.)

Step 16:
In a clean, dry mixing bowl, add mascarpone, vanilla extract, and Tia Maria, using a hand or stand mixer, medium speed, beat, until smooth and creamy.

Step 17:
Add 1/2 of coffee/espresso, then beat, until mixed well.

Step 18:
Transfer mixture to a bowl. Set aside.

Step 19:
In a clean, dry mixing bowl, add cream and 4 Tbsp confectioner's (powdered) sugar, then using hand or stand mixer, medium speed, until forms stiff peaks.

Checking for stiff peaks:
Stiff peaks are formed when you quickly dip the mixing beaters in and out once, pulling up some of the mixture into a peak, then it stays in the peak shape and does not fall down – like the topping of a meringue pie.

Step 20:
Add whipped cream to mascarpone mix, then gently fold to mix, taking care not to deflate the whipped cream. Set aside.

Step 21:

In a bowl, add remaining 1/2 coffee and remaining 1 Tbsp confectioner's sugar, then stir to mix well. Set aside.

Step 22:

For 1 martini glass, either break sponge cake into small pieces or use a section of cake to press and mold a "bowl" to line the glass – either way, first dip the sponge cake pieces / section into the coffee/sugar mix to evenly coat all sides, then add sponge cake to glass.

Step 23:

Add mascarpone mix, until reaches top of glass.

Step 24:

Using a grater or micro plane, add chocolate bar shavings, until have approximately 2 tsp on top of mascarpone mix.

Step 25:

Sprinkle to add cocoa powder on top of chocolate shavings.

Step 26:

Repeat Steps 22 – 26 for remaining martini glasses.

Step 27:

Transfer to refrigerator, to chill for 30 minutes.

Fresh Storage:

Cover with plastic wrap / film and store in the refrigerator. Use within 2 days.

Frozen Storage:

Cover dish with plastic wrap / film and store in freezer. Remove from freezer and place in refrigerator to thaw before use. May be frozen up to 2 weeks.

Your Notes:

_____

_____

Round One Guess As to the Inspirational Movie:

_____

MOVIE TWENTY-THREE

Level One Hint:

- The inspired dish is made by one Chef for another Chef who is not a dessert person, while they dine as if on Safari on the floor of the female Chef protagonist's apartment with her niece.

Round Two Guess As to the Inspirational Movie:

_____

MOVIE TWENTY-THREE

Level Two Hints:

- The female protagonist is the Chef at the upscale restaurant 22 Bleecker in Manhattan.
- The female protagonist makes food for Zoe while she is in the hospital but she refuses to eat it.
- Zoe and Nick make pancakes together, and Zoe, Kate, and Nick eventually open a restaurant of their own.
- Feed a man saffron sauce, and he might not move to San Francisco.
- Not just Chefs but all people should learn that recipes are similar to life in that you should create your own.

Round Three Guess As to the Inspirational Movie:

MOVIE TWENTY-THREE

Level Three Hints:

- Tiramisu
- The 2007 inspirational movie is based upon the story from a German movie originally titled Bella Martha from 2001, and this version was filmed in Brooklyn, NYC.
- Nick is the Sous Chef who plays opera in Chef Kate's kitchen, and who wears orange clog shoes like real-life Chef Mario Batalli.
- The inspirational film was directed by Scott Hicks, who used a Dolcetto wine in the film that is from his own wine label from his winery in South Australia, Yacca Paddock Vineyards.

Round Four Guess As to the Inspirational Movie:

_____

MOVIE TWENTY-FOUR

Course #1: Spaghetti Squash Fritters

Ingredients:

1 spaghetti-squash

2 tsp garlic, peeled, smashed, and minced

2 eggs

1/2 cup bread crumbs "Panko"

1/2 cup tomatoes, diced 1/4"

1/4 cup Parmesan cheese, grated

1 tsp Italian dried seasoning

1/2 tsp salt

1/8 tsp ground black pepper

1/4 cup olive oil

1/4 cup Parmesan cheese, grated

Directions:

Step 1:

Preheat oven to 400 degrees.

Step 2:

Cut squash in half lengthwise through stem and core.

473

Step 3:
Scoop out seeds.

Step 4:
In a baking pan, add squash, cut sides facing down and 2 cups of tap water.

Step 5:
Place pan in preheated oven, on the middle rack. Bake for 45 minutes, until soft.

Step 6:
Remove baking pan from oven and place on a heat-safe surface.

Step 7:
When cool enough to handle, pick up 1 half piece and hold over a bowl. Using a table fork, scrape through the soft inside of the squash, scraping lengthwise through a little at a time, creating long strands of squash which look like spaghetti pasta. Discard shell when done scraping.

Step 8:
Repeat Step 7 for the other half piece of squash.

Step 9:
Add garlic, eggs, Panko, tomatoes, parmesan, Italian seasoning, salt, and pepper, then stir to mix well.

Step 10:
Using bare hands, form and roll a portion of the squash mixture into a golf-ball-sized ball, then press to flatten to a disc 1/4" even thickness. Set aside.

Step 11:
Repeat Step 10 for all remaining squash mixture.

Step 12:
Stack 4 paper towels on a plate. Set aside.

Step 13:
In a pan, on medium heat, add oil and 1 squash mixture disc. Add additional discs as long as each sits side by side and does not touch the others.

Step 14:
Fry fritters 3 minutes, until golden-brown colored on the bottom sides.

Step 15:

Flip fritters over, then fry 3 minutes, until golden-brown colored on the bottom sides.

Step 16:

Remove fritters and place on prepared plate.

Step 17:

Repeat Steps 13 – 16, for all remaining squash mixture.

Step 18:

Sprinkle to add Parmesan cheese to fritters.

Fresh Storage:

Cover with plastic wrap / film and store in the refrigerator. Reheat in a pan. Use within 2 days.

Frozen Storage:

Do NOT freeze.

Your Notes:

_____

_____

MOVIE TWENTY-FOUR

Course #2: Brazilian Pan-Seared Steak served with Wild Mushroom Ragoût ("Rah-goo")

Wild Mushroom Ragoût Ingredients:

1 Tbsp butter

1 lb mixed fresh wild mushrooms, chopped into pieces of the same size

1/4 cup yellow onion, diced 1/4"

1 tsp garlic, peeled, smashed, and minced

3/4 cup chicken stock / broth

2 Tbsp demi-glace paste

1/3 cup dairy heavy whipping cream

1 tsp fresh thyme, stemmed

1 Tbsp chives, sliced 1/8"

1/2 tsp salt

1/8 tsp ground black pepper

Wild Mushroom Ragoût Directions:

Step 1:

In a pan, medium heat, add butter, mushrooms, and onion, then stir to mix. Cook for 5 minutes.

Step 2:

Add garlic, then stir to mix. Cook for 2 minutes.

Step 3:

Add chicken stock and demi-glace, then stir to mix well. Cook until simmering (almost boiling, but not at full boil).

Step 4:

Simmer for 7 minutes, stirring often.

Step 5:

Add cream, thyme, chives, salt, and pepper, then stir to mix well. Cook for 4 minutes.

Step 6:

Remove pan from heat, place on a heat-safe surface, such as a cold burner. Cover with lid to keep warm. Set aside.

Brazilian Pan-Seared Steak Ingredients:

1 Tbsp salt

1 tsp garlic powder

1 tsp onion powder

1/2 tsp ground black pepper

4 beef 9 oz steaks, cut of your choice

Brazilian Pan-Seared Steak Directions:

Step 1:

In a bowl, add salt, garlic powder, onion powder, and pepper, then stir to mix well.

Step 2:

Add steaks, then flip and move around in the seasoning to even coat all sides of the meat.

Step 3:

Transfer steaks to a pan (or grill if you prefer), medium heat, cook, flipping only once during cooking, until at desired doneness, according to internal temperature, checked with your thermometer.

Rare: 130-135   Medium Rare: 140

Medium: 155   Well Done: 165

Step 4:
Serve steak with ragout on the side.

Fresh Storage:
Cover ragoût with plastic wrap / film or place in a plastic sealable container and store in the refrigerator. Reheat in a pan. Use within 3 days.

Frozen Storage:
Do NOT freeze.

Your Notes:

_____

_____

MOVIE TWENTY-FOUR

Course #3: Blueberry "Caviar" served with Baked Brie

Ingredients:
1 small wheel of Brie cheese
2 Tbsp orange blossom honey
1 cup fresh blueberries

Directions:
Step 1:
Preheat oven to 350 degrees.

Step 2:
Place parchment paper sheet on a baking sheet / tray.

Step 3:
Add brie.

Step 4:
Place baking sheet in preheated oven, on the middle rack. Bake for 5 minutes.

Step 5:

Remove baking sheet and place on a heat-safe surface.

Step 6:

Add honey and fresh blueberries on top of brie.

Step 7:

Place baking sheet back in oven. Bake for 10 minutes.

Step 8:

Remove baking sheet and place on a heat-safe surface, such as your stovetop.

Step 9:

Portion into equal amounts on serving dishes.

Fresh / Frozen Storage:

Do NOT store.

Your Notes:

_____

Round One Guess As to the Inspirational Movie:

_____

MOVIE TWENTY-FOUR

Level One Hint:

- The inspired dish has a similar key ingredient as what was mentioned during a first class dinner where one of the male antagonists declines the dish being offered by the server as he does not like it.

Round Two Guess As to the Inspirational Movie:

_____

MOVIE TWENTY-FOUR

Level Two Hints:

- Chowder was served to the cast and crew on the final day of filming of the inspirational movie, but the food was laced with PCP ("angel dust"), sending over 80 people from the Nova Scotia set location to the local hospital.
- After the first class dinner scene from the inspirational movie scene, the men left the table to smoke cigars and drink brandy, leaving the women to drink tea.
- The third class passengers drank beer and danced late into the nights.

Round Three Guess As to the Inspirational Movie:

_____

MOVIE TWENTY-FOUR

Level Three Hints:

- Blueberry "Caviar" served with Baked Brie
- Real caviar was served in the first class dinner scene in the inspirational movie.
- The inspirational movie was originally called Planet Ice.
- "My Heart Will Go On", sung by Celine Dion, was used during the film's closing credits.
- James Cameron directed the inspirational movie and was the actual sketch artist for the scene with Rose reclining on the couch.
- You can steam up the windows in a car, even if it is parked on a boat.

Round Four Guess As to the Inspirational Movie:

_____

MOVIE TWENTY-FIVE

Course #1: Spring Rolls served with Peanut-Hoisin Sauce

Peanut-Hoisin Sauce Ingredients:

1/2 cup natural, creamy peanut butter

1/2 cup water

2 Tbsp Hoisin sauce (premade)

2 Tbsp San-G soya sauce

1 Tbsp honey

2 tsp chili garlic sauce (premade)

2 tsp lime juice

1/2 tsp sesame oil

Peanut-Hoisin Sauce Directions:

Step 1:

In a bowl, add peanut butter, water, Hoisin, soya sauce, honey, chili garlic sauce, lime juice, and sesame oil, then whisk to mix well, until a smooth sauce. Set aside.

Spring Rolls Ingredients:

1/2 cup rice vermicelli

1 red pepper, sliced 1/8" strips

1 cucumber, sliced 1/8" strips

1/2 cup bean sprouts

2 green onions, cut 1/8" pieces

1/4 cup carrot, grated

1 Tbsp San-G soya sauce

1 Tbsp sweet rice vinegar

2 Tbsp fresh cilantro, stemmed and chopped rough

2 Tbsp fresh basil, stemmed and chopped rough

1 package spring roll wrappers (premade)

hot tap water in a bowl

Spring Rolls Directions:

Step 1:

In a pot, on medium heat, bring 4 cups of water to boil.

Step 2:

Remove from heat and place on a heat-safe surface, such as a cold burner.

Step 3:

Add rice vermicelli, then stir.

Step 4:
Leave uncovered. Set aside 8 minutes, until soft.

Step 5:
Drain out water. Transfer to a bowl.

Step 6:
Add red pepper, cucumber, bean sprouts, green onions, carrot, soya sauce, rice vinegar, cilantro, and basil, then stir to mix well. Set aside.

Step 7:
Place bowl of hot water near a clean, dry, flat work surface.

Step 8:
Add 1 spring roll wrapper and using bare hands, hold until fully submerged for 5 seconds.

Step 9:
With bare hands, remove soft wrapper and lay flat on work surface.

Step 10:
Add 2 Tbsp to the center of the wrapper.

Step 11:
With both hands, grasp the wrapper edge closest to you, pull it over the filling and tuck edge underneath the filling, until snug.

Step 12:
Fold 1 side edge up, until snug against the filling roll, then lay flat on top of roll.

Step 13:
Repeat Step 12 for other side edge.

Step 14:
Gently roll the filled end toward the only open edge, until wrapper is fully rolled up to the edge. Set aside.

Step 15:
Repeat Steps 8 – 14 for all remaining rolls.

Step 16:
Serve spring rolls with peanut-hoisin sauce for dipping.

Fresh Storage:
Cover peanut-hoisin dipping sauce with plastic wrap / film and store in the refrigerator. Use within 5 days.

Cover spring rolls with plastic wrap / film and store in the refrigerator. Use within 1 day.

Frozen Storage:
Do NOT freeze.

Your Notes:

_____

_____

MOVIE TWENTY-FIVE

Course #2: Chinese-BBQ Pork

Basmati Rice: Frequently Used Side Item Recipes

Ingredients:

1 Tbsp garlic, peeled, smashed, and minced

2 Tbsp Chinese rice wine

2 Tbsp Hoisin sauce

2 Tbsp ketchup

1 & 1/2 Tbsp San-G soya sauce

1 Tbsp honey

2 tsp brown sugar

1/4 tsp Chinese five-spice powder

1 lb pork butt

1 tsp vegetable oil

1/4 tsp ginger, minced

1 baby bok choy, rinsed well, leaves separated from base

1/4 tsp salt

1 tsp vegetable oil

4 eggs

Directions:

Step 1:

In a bowl, add garlic, rice wine, Hoisin, ketchup, soya sauce, honey, brown sugar, and five-spice powder, then stir to mix well. Set aside.

Step 2:

Place pork on a cutting board. Cut pork butt into 1/4" slices, cutting against the grain of the meat.

Step 3:

Transfer pork slices to sauce bowl, then stir to coat slices well with sauce.

Step 4:

Cover with plastic wrap / film , then place in refrigerator to marinate for 4 hours.

Step 5:

Preheat oven to 350 degrees.

Step 6:

In a roasting pan, add 2 cups of water.

Step 7:

Place a roasting rack in the roasting pan.

Step 8:

Remove pork and marinade bowl and place on a work surface next to the roasting pan.

Step 9:

Transfer sliced pork onto the wire rack.

Step 10:

Place roasting pan in the preheated oven, on the middle rack. Bake 12 minutes, until internal temperature checks at 160 degrees with your thermometer.

Step 11:

Remove roasting pan from oven and place on a heat-safe surface. Set aside.

Step 12:

Prepare rice according to Frequently Used Side Item Recipe. Set aside.

Step 13:

In a pan, on medium heat, add marinade sauce, then bring to simmer (almost boiling, but not at full boil).

Step 14:

Remove pan from heat and place on heat-safe surface, such as a cold burner. Set aside.

Step 15:

In a pan, on medium heat, add oil, ginger, bok choy, and salt, then stir to mix well. Sauté 3 minutes.

Step 16:

Remove pan from heat and place on heat-safe surface, such as a cold burner. Set aside.

Step 17:

In a pan, preheat to medium heat.

Step 18:

Add oil and 2 eggs. Cook 2 minutes.

Step 19:

Flip eggs over gently, then cook 2 minutes.

Step 20:
With spatula, transfer eggs to a plate.

Step 21:
Repeat Steps 18 – 20 for remaining two eggs.

Step 22: Assemble equal portions into bowls: rice, then pork, then bok choy, and then an egg.

Step 23:
Serve with the warm marinade as additional sauce.

Fresh Storage:
Cover extra pork and marinade with plastic wrap / film and store in the refrigerator. Use within 3 days.

Frozen Storage:
Cover extra pork with plastic wrap / film or place in a plastic sealable bag, and store in freezer. Remove from freezer and place in refrigerator to thaw before use. Reheat in a pan. May be frozen up to 4 weeks.

Your Notes:

MOVIE TWENTY-FIVE

Course #3: New Year Cookies

Ingredients:
4 cups roasted peanuts, ground

1 cup powdered sugar

1 cup peanut oil

2 cups flour

2 Tbsp vegetable shortening (Crisco)

1 egg

Directions:
Step 1:

Preheat oven to 350 degrees.

Step 2:

In a bowl, add peanuts, sugar, peanut oil, flour, and shortening, then stir to mix well into dough.

Step 3:

Place 1 Tbsp into bare hands, then form and roll into a ball.

Step 4:
Place ball on a baking sheet.

Step 5:
Using a table fork, lightly press down once on the top of the ball to flatten it into a disc that is 1/2 of the original ball height.

Step 6:
Repeat Steps 3 – 5 for all remaining dough.

Step 7:
In a bowl, add egg, then whisk, until light and creamy.

Step 8:
Using a pastry brush, gently coat the tops of the dough discs with the whisked egg.

Step 9:
Place baking sheet in the preheated oven, on the middle rack. Bake for 20 minutes, until golden-brown colored.

Step 10:
Remove baking sheet from oven and place on a heat-safe surface.

Step 11:
Transfer cookies to a wire rack to cool 10 minutes.

Fresh Storage:
Place in a plastic sealable bag or container and store in the refrigerator. Use within 14 days.

Frozen Storage:
Place in a plastic sealable bag or container, and store in freezer. Remove from freezer and place on countertop to thaw. May be frozen up to 3 months.

Your Notes:

_____

_____

Round One Guess As to the Inspirational Movie:

_____

MOVIE TWENTY-FIVE

Level One Hint:

- The inspired dish is made by a cook named Turkey, who serves it to the protagonist, who is lying down in an alley and is famished after being beaten up.

Round Two Guess As to the Inspirational Movie:

_____

MOVIE TWENTY-FIVE

Level Two Hints:

- Two vendors, Goosehead and Turkey, argue over which one gets to serve the Beef Balls and "Pissing" Shrimp dishes.

- In a cooking competition, make sure that your "Buddha Jumping Wall" does not explode.

- The dish prepared at the end of the film may make you sorrowful.

- The protagonist critiques Assorted Noodles by challenging each ingredient.

- Following your heart to expose emotions will also reveal excellence in cooking.

Round Three Guess As to the Inspirational Movie:

_____

MOVIE TWENTY-FIVE

Level Three Hints:

- Chinese-BBQ Pork
- Released in 1996, this Hong Kong comedy is also known as Sik San.
- While in a monastery, the protagonist learns from Wet Dream about both cooking and Kung Fu.
- Watch out for the 18 Bronzemen and practice your chair technique while watching the inspirational movie.

Round Four Guess As to the Inspirational Movie:

_____

MOVIE TWENTY-SIX

Course #1: Veggie Antipasti Zucchini Boats

Pickled Onion Ingredients:
1 cup red onion, sliced thinly
1/2 cup red-wine vinegar
1/2 cup warm water (80 – 100 degrees)
1 tsp sugar
1/4 tsp salt

Pickled Onion Directions:
Step 1:
In a bowl, add onion, vinegar, and water. Stir to mix.

Step 2:
Add sugar and salt, then stir to mix well. Set aside 30 minutes.

Step 3:
Cover with plastic wrap / film and place in refrigerator to chill, until ready to use. Use within 2 days.

Boat Ingredients:

4 medium-sized zucchini, sliced in half lengthwise, seeded
   center scooped out with spoon

1/3 cup tap water

Boat Directions:

Step 1:

Preheat oven to 375 degrees.

Step 2:

In a pan, add zucchini, cut side facing up. Add water.

Step 3:

Place baking pan in preheated oven, on the middle rack.
Bake for 30 minutes.

Step 4:

Remove baking pan and place on heat-safe surface. Set
aside.

Vinaigrette Ingredients:

3 Tbsp red-wine vinegar

1 tsp garlic, peeled, smashed, and minced

1/2 tsp sugar

1/2 tsp salt

1/8 tsp ground black pepper

6 Tbsp extra-virgin olive oil

Vinaigrette Directions:

Step 1:

In a bowl, add vinegar, garlic, sugar, salt, and pepper then whisk well. While whisking vigorously and continuously, slowly drizzle in oil to form an emulsion. Set aside.

Filling Ingredients:

1/2 cup pickled onions

1/2 cup fresh flat-leaf parsley leaves

4 oz jar roasted red peppers, rinsed, drained, and cut lengthwise into 1/4" strips

6 oz jar marinated artichoke hearts, drained and chopped

1/2 cup assorted brine-cured olives, cut in half

1/2 cup bottled pepperoncini, drained and chopped

1/2 cup cherry tomatoes, cut in half

Filling Directions:

Step 1:

In a bowl add onions, parsley, red pepper, artichoke hearts, olives, pepperoncini, and cherry tomatoes, then stir to mix.

Step 2:

Add Vinaigrette, then stir to mix well.

Step 3:

Transfer 1/8 of filling into 1 zucchini boat. Set aside on a serving plate.

Step 4:

Repeat Step 3 for all remaining filling and boats.

Step 5:

Drizzle to add leftover Vinaigrette equally over boats.

Fresh/Frozen Storage:

Do NOT store.

Your Notes:

MOVIE TWENTY-SIX

Course #2: Pizza Napoletana

Crust Ingredients: (makes 2 large pizzas)
4 & 1/2 cups bread flour

1 & 1/4 tsp active dry yeast

2 cups water, chilled

1 & 3/4 tsp salt

2 Tbsp olive oil

Crust Directions:

Step 1:

In a bowl, add flour, yeast, and water, then stir to mix well.

Step 2:

Add salt, then stir to mix well.

Step 3:

Cover the bowl with plastic wrap / film and transfer to refrigerator for a minimum of 8 hours. Dough can be kept waiting for up to 3 days.

Step 4:
Transfer bowl from refrigerator to countertop and set aside for 2 hours at room temperature.

Step 5:
Preheat oven to 450 degrees. If you have a baking stone, preheat the stone in the oven.

Step 6:
Knead 2 to 3 minutes. Do not use a mixer.

Step 7:
Do not clean the flour from the countertop after kneading. If the flour was used up during kneading, then reapply flour dusting to the countertop.

Step 8:
Cut dough in half.

(*Storage for other half)

Step 9:

Place 1 half-dough on the floured surface and using a rolling pin, press down and roll out in different directions over and over until you have even thickness and becomes a rectangle approximately 12 x 17".

Step 10:

Using a pastry brush, brush olive oil on one side gently and lightly. You do not have to use all the oil. Transfer shaped dough to a half-sheet pan or baking / pizza stone, placing the oil side down. Set aside.

Tomato Sauce Ingredients:

28 oz high quality canned whole tomatoes (do not drain)
1/4 tsp ground black pepper
1/2 tsp salt
1 tsp dried oregano

Tomato Sauce Directions:

Step 1:

To a blender or food processor, add tomatoes with juice, pepper, salt, and oregano, then blend, until smooth. Set aside.

Pizza Assembly Ingredients:

1 lb fresh mozzarella, sliced 1/4 " slices

12 fresh basil leaves, stemmed and torn

ground black pepper, to taste

Pizza Assembly Directions:

Step 1:

To pizza dough, add tomato sauce, then spread for a thin layer of even thickness.

Step 2:

Add mozzarella, with equal distribution and according to preference for amount used (less can be more).

Step 3:

Place the pan / pre-heated stone into the preheated oven, on the middle rack. Bake for 10 to 15 minutes, until cheese is golden-brown colored and pizza is done to your preference.

Step 4:

Remove the pizza from the oven and place the pan / stone on heat-safe surface, such as your stovetop.

Step 5:
Sprinkle to add basil.

Fresh Storage:

Once cooled to room temperature, cover the pizza with plastic wrap / film or place in a plastic sealable bag and store in the refrigerator. May reheat in the oven on a half-sheet pan / pizza stone uncovered. Use within 3 days.

Frozen Storage:

Once cooled to room temperature, cover the pizza with plastic wrap / film or place in a plastic sealable bag, move to refrigerator until completely cooled, then move to freezer. Remove from freezer and place on countertop to thaw before use. May reheat in the oven on a half-sheet pan / pizza stone uncovered. May be frozen up to 1 month.

*Storing the other half-dough piece for a pizza later on:

Choice 1: Transfer the half-dough piece back into the bowl and cover it with plastic wrap / film, transfer the covered bowl to the refrigerator, then keep for up to 3 days from date that you did Step 1. To use, transfer the bowl to countertop and allow to come to room temperature, then preheat oven to 450 degrees, dust flour on the countertop area, then move on to Step 9 in the pizza crust directions.

Choice 2: Roll out the half-dough piece as described in Step 9, transfer shaped dough to a half-sheet pan, cover pan with plastic wrap / film, transfer covered pan to freezer, then keep for up to 2 weeks from date that you did Step 1. To thaw, transfer pan to countertop, remove dough to countertop, and allow dough to come to room temperature, then preheat oven to 450 degrees, then move on to Step 10 in the pizza crust directions.

Your Notes:

_____

_____

MOVIE TWENTY-SIX

Course #3: White Russian Pie

Crust Ingredients:

1 cup flour

1/2 tsp salt

1/4 cup solid vegetable shortening (Crisco)

2 Tbsp butter, softened

2 & 1/2 Tbsp ice water (in a glass, put ice cubes into
   cold tap water for several minutes and portion out
   the measurement needed just before using)

2 cups of either dry rice or dry beans – any kind

Crust Directions:

Step 1:

Preheat oven to 350 degrees.

Step 2:

In a bowl, add flour, salt, shortening, butter, and water,
then knead the dough with your hands until it begins to
stick together as a ball.

If the ball does not form well, then knead a bit more and try to form the ball again. (You may need to add additional ice-cold water to make the mixture sticky enough to form the ball, but only add a little water at a time, kneading the water in before adding more.)

Step 3:
Cover the dough with plastic wrap / film and place in refrigerator to chill for 30 minutes.

Step 4:
Prepare an area to roll out your crust, such as a countertop or table, cleaning and drying the area well, then scattering a little flour on that surface a little bigger than the size that your crust needs to be.

Step 5:
Place the chilled dough ball on the floured surface and using a rolling pin, press down and roll out in different directions over and over until you have even thickness and enough surface area to fit your deep pie plate. You can do an approximate measurement by holding the plate over the dough to see if the dough is bigger than the pie plate by at least 2".

Step 6:
Gently lift one edge of your dough to fold the dough circle in half, then carefully move the entire circle of dough onto your pie plate, adjusting to cover one half and having some overlapping the plate edge, then unfold the circle to cover the entire pie plate and have some dough overlapping all of the pie plate edges.

Step 7:
Gently press the dough so that it lies against the sides of the pie plate. Run a knife along the outer edge of the pie plate to trim off the excess dough.

Step 8:
Place the pointer finger and thumb of one hand together with the finger pads touching each other, then place the combined fingertips at the outer edge of the plate aiming into the center and use the pointer finger of your other hand to push the edge of the dough into the point formed by the combined fingers. Move around the edge of the dough repeating this until you have "fluted" the entire circle of dough for the edge of the pie crust.

Step 9:
Gently place 1 piece of aluminum foil on the bottom of the pan, covering the dough.

Step 10:
Add 2 cups of either dry rice or dry beans, spreading until these are in a single layer on the foil. These will hold down the foil and thus the crust, not allowing the crust to expand too much during baking.

Step 11:
Place the pie pan in the preheated oven, on the middle rack. Bake for 15 minutes.

Step 12:
Remove beans / rice and foil. Bake another 10 minutes, until light golden-brown colored.

Step 13:
Remove pie pan and place on a wire rack to cool before filling.

(*Storage for beans / rice)

Filling Ingredients:

3/4 cup whole (3%) dairy milk

1 & 1/4 oz packet of unflavored gelatin

4 eggs, separated, then placed in separate bowls

1/4 cup sugar

4 Tbsp sugar

1/2 tsp instant coffee powder

1/3 cup Kahlua

1/8 cup Vodka

1/2 cup dairy heavy whipping cream

Step 1:

In a large bowl, fill halfway with ice and cold water, making an "ice bath". This needs to be big enough to hold the metal bowl from Step 7. Set aside.

Step 2:

In a pot, on medium heat, add milk, and gelatin, then stir to mix well and wait for gelatin to be absorbed by the milk.

Step 3:
Add egg yolks, sugar, and instant coffee, then stir to mix well. Cook for 12 minutes, stirring frequently.

Step 4:
Do not allow to boil. The mix will thicken, and the sugar will be dissolved.

Step 5:
Remove pot from heat and place on a heat-safe surface, such as a cold burner.

Step 6:
Add Kahlua and vodka, then stir to mix well.

Step 7:
Transfer to a metal bowl.

Step 8:
Place metal bowl in the prepared "ice bath" bowl.

Step 9:
Stir frequently, until the mix is cool to the touch.

Step 10:
Remove metal bowl from ice bath bowel and place on a towel on a flat work surface.

Step 11:
Carefully dry the outside of the bowl with the towel.

Step 12:
Cover with plastic wrap / film and place in refrigerator to chill while continuing on to Step 13.

Step 13:
In a mixing bowl, add egg whites, then using a hand or stand mixer, on medium speed, beat, until frothy.

Step 14:
Increase to high speed. Add sugar, 1 Tbsp at a time, then continue beating, until holds stiff peaks. Set aside.

Checking for stiff peaks:
Stiff peaks are formed when you quickly dip the mixing beaters in and out once, pulling up some of the mixture into a peak, then it stays in the peak shape and does not fall down – like the topping of a meringue pie.

Step 15:
Remove chilled bowl from refrigerator.

Step 16:
Add mixing bowl contents, gently folding, taking care to not deflate the mixture.

Step 17:
Recover and place in refrigerator to chill while continuing on to Step 18.

Step 18:
Carefully clean the mixing bowl and beaters.

Step 19:
In a mixing bowl, add the heavy cream, then using a hand or stand mixer, on high speed, beat, until holds stiff peaks. Set aside.

Checking for stiff peaks:
Stiff peaks are formed when you quickly dip the mixing beaters in and out once, pulling up some of the mixture into a peak, then it stays in the peak shape and does not fall down – like the topping of a meringue pie.

Step 20:
Remove chilled bowl from refrigerator.

Step 21:
Add mixing bowl contents, gently folding, taking care to not deflate the mixture.

Step 22:
Using a spatula / spoon, transfer to prepared pie crust, spreading evenly.

Step 23:
Cover with plastic wrap / film and place in refrigerator to chill while continuing on to whipped cream element.

Whipped Cream Ingredients:
1/2 cup dairy heavy whipping cream
2 Tbsp cocoa powder
2 Tbsp sugar (recommend a vanilla sugar)

Whipped Cream Directions:
Step 1:
Carefully clean the mixing bowl and beaters.

Step 2:

In a mixing bowl, add the heavy cream, cocoa powder, and sugar, then using a hand or stand mixer, on high speed, beat, until holds stiff peaks.

Checking for stiff peaks:

Stiff peaks are formed when you quickly dip the mixing beaters in and out once, pulling up some of the mixture into a peak, then it stays in the peak shape and does not fall down – like the topping of a meringue pie.

Step 3:

With spatula / spoon, add whipped topping to top of pie, gently distributing over all of pie filling, taking care to not deflate the filling or topping.

Step 4:

Cover loosely with plastic wrap / film or place a plastic or glass "dome" over the pie and store in the refrigerator. You can use toothpicks inserted in just far enough to keep upright then "tent" the plastic wrap / film overtop to keep it from touching the pie and disturbing the whipped cream topping. Chill for at least 2 hours before serving.

Fresh Storage:

Cover loosely with plastic wrap / film or place a plastic or glass "dome" over the pie and store in the refrigerator. You can use toothpicks inserted in just far enough to keep upright then "tent" the plastic wrap / film overtop to keep it from touching the pie and disturbing the whipped cream topping. Use within 3 days.

Frozen Storage:
Do NOT freeze.

Storage for Dried Beans / Rice:
You can use these multiple times and with baking crusts of different types, so store these in a sealable plastic bag or container out of direct sunlight or heat, such as a pantry or dry goods cupboard.

Your Notes:

_____

_____

Round One Guess As to the Inspirational Movie:

_____

Lisa Shipley and James Shipley

MOVIE TWENTY-SIX

Level One Hint:

- In 2010, the female protagonist inspired this dish while she learned to forsake taking self-loathing into the shower and to buy bigger jeans for her muffin-top during her time in Napoli.

Round Two Guess As to the Inspirational Movie:

_____

MOVIE TWENTY-SIX

Level Two Hints:

- The female protagonist is nicknamed Groceries.
- If you find a barbershop in Rome, then see if a man named Luca Spaghetti is in there and will be your tour guide.
- Directed by Ryan Murphy and based upon a memoir by Liz Gilbert, the inspirational movie gave women permission to eat and have a healthy appetite, especially during Liz's pasta-eating scene where she showed unabashed enjoyment of her meal with no distractions.

Round Three Guess As to the Inspirational Movie:

_____

MOVIE TWENTY-SIX

Level Three Hints:

- Pizza Napoletana
- Liz is like most of us when we try to meditate, easily distracted by details and random thoughts.
- We are all men and women in search of a word that defines who we are, not what we do.
- If you too set out on a journey to help yourself, sometimes you would help "Tutti" (everybody), just like Liz did.

Round Four Guess As to the Inspirational Movie:

MOVIE TWENTY-SEVEN

Course #1: Mushroom Soup

Ingredients:

1/2 cup butter

1 lb fresh wild mushrooms, cut 1/8 " pieces

1/2 lb button mushrooms, minced

3 shallots, minced

1/2 cup dry sherry

3 cups vegetable stock / broth

1 tsp garlic, peeled, smashed, and minced

1 tsp salt

1/4 tsp ground black pepper

2/3 cup crème fraîche

Directions:

Step 1:

In a pan, on medium heat, add butter and shallots, then stir to mix. Cook, until shallot is translucent.

Step 2:
Add all mushrooms, then stir to mix. Cook for 10 - 15
minutes, until mushrooms have released most of the water
content.

Step 3:
Add sherry, stock, garlic, salt, and pepper, then stir to
mix. Bring to simmer (almost boiling but not at full boil).

Step 4:
Simmer for 15 minutes.

Step 5:
Remove pan from heat and place on a heat-safe surface,
such as a cold burner. (*Frozen Storage)

Step 6:
Add crème fraîche, then stir to mix well.

Step 7:
Add salt and pepper, to taste, then stir to mix well.

Fresh Storage:

Cover with plastic wrap / film or place in a plastic sealable container and store in the refrigerator. Reheat in a pan. Use within 3 days.

Frozen Storage:

If stop after Step 5 completed, then with plastic wrap / film or place in a plastic sealable container, and store in freezer. Remove from freezer and place in refrigerator to thaw before use continuing on to Step 6. Reheat in a pan. May be frozen up to 4 weeks.

Your Notes:

_____

_____

MOVIE TWENTY-SEVEN

Course #2: Shepherd's Pie

Ingredients:

2 Tbsp olive oil

1 lb lean lamb, minced

1 tsp salt

1/2 tsp ground black pepper

1 cup yellow onion, grated finely

1/2 cup carrot, grated finely

1 Tbsp garlic, peeled, smashed, and minced

3 Tbsp Worcestershire sauce

1 Tbsp tomato puree

2 tsp fresh thyme, stemmed and chopped

2 tsp fresh rosemary, stemmed and chopped

1 cup red wine

1 cup chicken stock / broth

3 lbs potatoes, peeled and diced 2" pieces

6 Tbsp butter

2 eggs, separated and yolks kept

1/2 cup Parmesan, grated

salt

ground black pepper

Directions:

Step 1:

Preheat oven to 350 degrees.

Step 2:

In pan, on medium heat, add oil and lamb.

Step 3:

Sprinkle to add salt and pepper, then stir to mix. Cook 4 minutes, until lamb begins to brown.

Step 4:

Add onion, carrot, and garlic, then stir to mix well. Cook, until onion begins to turn translucent.

Step 5:

Add Worcestershire sauce, tomato puree, thyme, rosemary, wine, and chicken stock, then stir to mix well. Cook, until the lamb is no longer sitting in liquid but still very moist.

Step 6:

Transfer to an 8 x 8" baking pan. Set aside.

Step 7:
In a pot, on high heat, add potatoes and enough cold water to cover the potatoes by 3".

Step 8:
Add salt, so that when you taste the water with a spoon, you can clearly taste salt. Boil 30 minutes, until soft enough to easily pierce with a fork.

Step 9:
Drain the water.

Step 10:
Add butter, yolks, and parmesan, then with a hand masher or hand mixer, mash, until light and fluffy.

Step 11:
Add salt and pepper, to taste, then stir to mix well.

Step 12:
Transfer to the baking pan, placing on top of the meat so as not to reduce fluffiness of potatoes.

Step 13:
Place baking pan in the preheated oven, on the middle rack. Bake for 20 minutes, until golden-brown colored and bubbly.

Step 14:
Remove baking pan and place on a heat-safe surface, such as your stovetop.

Step 15:
Cool 5 minutes, before serving.

Fresh Storage:
Cover dish with plastic wrap / film and store in the refrigerator. Reheat in a pan. Use within 3 days.

Frozen Storage:
Cover dish with plastic wrap / film or place in a plastic sealable bag, and store in freezer. Remove from freezer and place in refrigerator to thaw before use. Reheat in a pan. May be frozen up to 2 weeks.

Your Notes:

MOVIE TWENTY-SEVEN

Course #3: Chocolate Digestive Biscuit with Builder's Tea

Ingredients:

1/2 cup old-fashioned rolled oats

1 & 1/2 cups whole wheat flour

1/2 cup flour

1/2 tsp salt

1 tsp baking powder

1/2 cup butter, diced 1/2 "

3/4 cup confectioner's (powdered) sugar

1/4 cup whole (3%) dairy milk

6 oz milk chocolate (bar)

black tea

milk, to taste

sugar, to taste (typically 2 tsp per mug)

Equipment:

a bain marie / a double boiler / OR a metal mixing bowl
    with a rim that is bigger around than a pot so that
    the bowl can sit on top of the pot and allow the
    bottom of the bowl to rest just above the water
    level in the pot.

Directions:

Step 1:
Preheat oven to 350 degrees.

Step 2:
Line 2 baking sheets with parchment paper. Set aside.

Step 3:
Sprinkle flour on a flat, clean, dry work surface. Set
aside.

Step 4:
In a blender or food processor, add oats. Blend for 5
seconds.

Step 5:
Add whole wheat flour, flour, salt, and baking powder.
Blend for 5 seconds.

Step 6:
Add butter. Blend, until there are no chunks of butter
larger than 1/8".

Step 7:
Add sugar and milk. Blend, until the mix is uniform in
appearance.

Step 8:
On the floured work surface, using a rolling pin, press
down and roll out from the center of the dough ball, over
and over, each time rolling in a different direction, until
you roll out an 1/8" circle of even thickness.

Step 9:
Using a cookie cutter OR a drinking glass, gently make
2 - 3" circles by pressing the cookie cutter straight down
all the way through the dough. (Do not twist!)

Step 10:
Using a spatula, remove cut-out circles, transfer to prepared baking sheets, leaving 1/2" empty space all around each circle of dough.

Step 11:
Place baking sheets in the preheated oven, on racks set equally apart from the center position. Bake 18 - 22 minutes, until golden-brown colored.

Step 12:
In a pot, medium heat, add water, about 1" deep, until just below where metal bowl will rest when placed on top of the pot. Set aside.

Step 13:
In the metal bowl, add chocolate, then place on top of the pot.

Step 14:
Stir until chocolate melts completely.

Step 15:
Remove bowl and place on a heat-safe surface, such as a cold burner.

Step 16:
In the metal bowl, dip 1 flat-side of 1 cookie in the chocolate.

Step 17:
Use a spatula or frosting knife to spread chocolate across flat side, until evenly coated.

Step 18:
Place cookie on a wire rack to cool. Set aside.

Step 19:
Repeat Steps 16 – 18 for all remaining cookies.

Step 20:
Prepare a hot black tea of your preference, in your preferred method, steeping extra-long to produce a strong tea.

Step 21:
Add milk and sugar, to taste.

Step 22:
Serve biscuits with tea for dunking.

Fresh Storage:
Cover biscuits with plastic wrap / film or place in a plastic sealable bag and store in the refrigerator. Use within 5 days.

Frozen Storage:
Cover biscuits with plastic wrap / film or place in a plastic sealable bag, and store in freezer. Remove from freezer and place in refrigerator to thaw before use. May be frozen up to 2 weeks.

Your Notes:

_____

_____

Round One Guess As to the Inspirational Movie:

_____

MOVIE TWENTY-SEVEN

Level One Hint:

- Evelyn advises in a call center and on calculating the method and timing to use when eating this inspired dish.

Round Two Guess As to the Inspirational Movie:

MOVIE TWENTY-SEVEN

Level Two Hints:

- Jean thinks that ham sandwiches have germs and that BLTs are made with bacteria, not bacon.
- Jean never accepts any of the local food, the new city that her husband explores, or her husband's plan to return to England with her.
- At first, Muriel will not eat any type of food that she cannot pronounce, but Muriel comes to accept the untouchable cleaning girl and the food that she offers to Muriel.

Round Three Guess As to the Inspirational Movie:

_____

MOVIE TWENTY-SEVEN

Level Three Hints:

- Chocolate Digestive Biscuit with Builder's Tea
- The 2004 novel "The Foolish Things" by Deborah Moggach was adapted into the 2012 British Comedy-Drama inspirational film.
- Set in England and in Jaipur, India, these seven principals may be retired but still have a lot to learn.
- Bill Nighy and Penelope Wilton have played a married couple in another film, Shaun of the Dead.
- Apple Tobacco lands Douglas in an evening to remember or not to.

Round Four Guess As to the Inspirational Movie:

_____

MOVIE TWENTY-EIGHT

Course #1: Cucumber & Goat Cheese Bites

Ingredients:
2 English seedless cucumbers, sliced 1" pieces
1 heirloom tomato, diced 1/4"
4 oz package herbed garlic goat cheese
4 cherry peppers, diced 1/4"

Directions:
Step 1:
Hold 1 cucumber slice flat in your bare hand, 1 cut-side facing up, then using a spoon, carve a deep bowl-shape in the middle of the slice. Set aside.

Step 2:
Repeat Step 1 for all remaining cucumber slices.

Step 3:
In a bowl, add goat cheese, then whisk, until creamy.

Step 4:
Add tomato, then stir to mix.

Step 5:
Hold 1 cucumber slice flat in your bare hand, bowl-side facing up, then using a spoon, add mixture to fill "bowl". Set aside on a serving plate.

Step 6:
Repeat Step 5 for all remaining cucumber slices.

Step 7:
Sprinkle to add cherry pepper pieces to top of filled "bowls", evenly distributing over all.

Fresh Storage:
Cover with plastic wrap / film and store in the refrigerator. Use within 1 day.

Frozen Storage:
Do NOT freeze.

Your Notes:

MOVIE TWENTY-EIGHT

Course #2: Ratatouille

Ingredients:

2 Tbsp extra virgin olive oil

1 Tbsp garlic, peeled, smashed, and minced

1 yellow onion, minced

1 red pepper, diced 1/8"

1 yellow pepper, diced 1/8"

1 orange pepper, diced 1/8"

30 oz canned tomatoes, drained and diced 1/8"

2 sprigs thyme, stemmed and chopped

2 Tbsp balsamic vinegar

4 roma tomatoes, sliced 1/8"

2 zucchini, sliced 1/8"

2 yellow squash, sliced 1/8"

1 eggplant, peeled and sliced 1/8"

1 tsp salt

1/4 tsp ground black pepper

nonstick olive oil cooking spray

Directions:

Step 1:

In a pan, on medium heat, add oil, garlic, onion, and all peppers, then stir to mix. Cook 4 minutes, stirring constantly.

Step 2:

Add drained tomatoes and thyme, then stir to mix well. Bring to simmer (almost boiling but not at full boil).

Step 3:

Remove from heat and place on a heat-safe surface, such as a cold burner.

Step 4:

Add balsamic vinegar, then stir to mix well. Set aside.

Step 5:

In a 9x13" baking pan, spray olive oil to coat pan inside.

Step 6:

Add 1/2 cup of sauce, then spread across bottom of pan.

Step 7:

Process: Starting in one corner, lay down a slice tomato. Keeping in the same row, on top of it, lay down a slice of zucchini, leaving 1/8" of the tomato showing. Keeping in the same row, on top of that, lay down a slice of squash, leaving 1/8" of the zucchini showing. Keeping in the same row, on top of that, lay down a slice of eggplant, leaving 1/8" of the squash showing. Keeping in the same row, lay down a slice of tomato, leaving 1/8" of the eggplant showing. Keep overlapping in this row the sequence of tomato, zucchini, squash, and eggplant, until get to the opposite corner of the row.

Step 8:

Create a row next to the first one, following the same process as described in Step 7.

Step 9:

Keep creating rows of overlapping vegetable slices as described in Step 7, until the bottom of the pan is covered.

Step 10:
Sprinkle to add salt and pepper evenly over the rows of layered vegetables.

Step 11:
Using a spoon, add all of the remaining sauce, over the top of the layered vegetables, evenly distributed.

Step 12:
Cover pan in aluminum foil, making sure to not let the foil touch the contents of the pan.

Step 13:
Place the baking pan in the preheated oven, on the middle rack. Bake for 2 hours.

Step 14:
Remove baking pan and place on a heat-safe surface, such as your stovetop. Uncover pan.

Step 15:
Place the baking pan back in the preheated oven, on the middle rack. Bake 20 minutes.

Step 16:
Remove baking pan from oven and place on a heat-safe surface, such as your stovetop.

Fresh Storage:
Cover pan with plastic wrap / film and store in the refrigerator. Reheat in the pan. Use within 3 days.

Frozen Storage:
Do NOT freeze.

Your Notes:

_____

_____

MOVIE TWENTY-EIGHT

Course #3: Chocolate Cake with Chocolate Frosting

Cake Ingredients:

2 cups sugar

1 & 3/4 cup flour

3/4 cup cocoa

1 tsp salt

1 & 1/2 tsp baking powder

1 & 1/2 tsp baking soda

2 eggs, beaten

1/2 cup canola oil

1 cup whole (3%) dairy milk

1 cup boiling water

2 round 9" cake pans

parchment paper sheets

Cake Directions:

Step 1:

Lightly coat 2 round 9" cake pans with non-stick vegetable cooking oil spray.

Step 2:

Place a round cake pan onto parchment paper, then use a pencil to trace around the pan.

Step 3:

Repeat tracing until 2 circles have been made on the paper.

Step 4:

Using kitchen scissors / shears, cut parchment paper just inside of the traced line so as to avoid having any pencil mark on the circles when done being cut out. Use scissors that are only used in the kitchen for food use; do not use household scissors.

Step 5:

Place a parchment paper circle into each cake pan. Lightly coat parchment paper circles with non-stick vegetable cooking oil spray.

Step 6:

Preheat oven to 350 degrees.

Step 7:
In a bowl, add flour, cocoa, salt, baking powder, and baking soda, then stir to mix well.

Step 8:
Add eggs and oil, then stir to mix well.

Step 9:
Add milk, then stir to mix well.

Step 10:
(note: once you do this step, move quickly until the pans are in the oven, as the hot water is going to start baking the batter in this step!)
Add hot water, then stir to mix well. The batter will look very soupy, this is normal.

Step 11:
Transfer batter in equal amounts to the 2 prepared cake pans.

Step 12:
Place the pans in the preheated oven, on the middle rack, side by side. Bake for 30 - 35 minutes.

Step 13:

When done, cake will pull away from edges of pan all the way around.

Check at the center of the cake, with a toothpick inserted straight down and for approximately 3/4 the length of the toothpick, then wiggle the toothpick a bit to make a hole large enough to not scrape the edges of the toothpick as it is removed. If done, then the toothpick should be "clean" or dry after removed, without wet batter sticking to it. (If not "clean", then bake a few minutes more and recheck. Repeat until "clean".)

Step 14:

Remove cake pans from oven and place on a wire rack to cool, for 5 minutes.

Step 15:

Insert a thin-blade knife along the inner edge of a cake pan. "Run" the knife all along the inner edge to separate the cake from the pan edges. Invert the pan over the wire rack, allowing the cake to leave the pan and lay on the wire rack to cool.

Step 16:
Carefully, peel off the parchment circle and discard it.

Step 17:
Repeat Steps 15 & 16 for the other cake pan.

Step 18:
Set aside for at least 20 minutes at room temperature, until cool enough to frost.

Frosting Ingredients:
1/3 cup sugar
1 cup dairy heavy whipping cream
2 oz butter
10 oz dark chocolate bar (86+%), chopped rough

Frosting Directions:
Step 1:
In a pot, on medium heat, add cream and sugar, then whisk, until mixed well.

Step 2:
Cook, until you see the first bubble, then remove from heat and place on a heat-safe surface, like a cold burner.

Step 3:
Add butter and chopped chocolate, then stir, until no pieces of butter or chocolate remain and mixed well.

Step 4:
Set aside, to cool 10 minutes, until frosting is thick enough to spread.

Cake Assembly and Frosting:
Step 1:
Place 1 cooled cake layer on a serving plate or cake stand.

Step 2:
Using a frosting "knife" (rounded tip and not sharp) OR a frosting/pastry spatula, place a large dollop (about 1/3 cup) of frosting in the middle of the top of the cake layer.

Step 3:
Using frosting knife, stay in touch with the frosting to spread it from the middle to cover the cake layer to the edges. Do not touch the cake surface directly with the frosting knife. Make the frosting fairly level, adding more frosting if needed.

Note:
The first frosting is considered as a "crumb coat": a thin layer of frosting meant to keep crumbs from getting in the final frosting layer, so do not worry if this thin layer has crumbs mixed in – it will be covered later.

Note:
Frosting for a 2 layer cake should be divided in 4 equal parts. 1/4 goes between the bottom and top layers. 1/4 goes over the top layer. 1/2 goes on the top and sides of the 2 layers.

Step 4:
Place the second cake layer on the first, then repeat Step 2 & 3 to frost a crumb coat on the top of it.

Step 5:
Place several smaller dollops of frosting at equally spaced intervals on the edges of the top layer.

Step 6:
Use these dollops to pull frosting down the sides of the cake, still keeping the frosting knife only in contact with frosting as you move around and combining areas to fully cover the side of the cake all around.

Step 7:
Set aside for 5 minutes to allow the crumb coat to "set".

Step 8:
Place all remaining frosting on the top of the cake, then using frosting knife, spread the final coat of frosting on the top and sides of the cake, until evenly spread.

Fresh Storage:

Cover loosely with plastic wrap / film or place a plastic or glass "dome" over the cake and store in the refrigerator. You can use toothpicks inserted in just far enough to keep upright then "tent" the plastic wrap / film overtop to keep it from touching the cake and disturbing the frosting. Use within 5 days.

Frozen Storage:

Do NOT freeze.

Your Notes:

_____

_____

Round One Guess As to the Inspirational Movie:

_____

MOVIE TWENTY-EIGHT

Level One Hint:

- The inspired dish is served when the anthropomorphic Remy and the female antagonist, Colette, prove Chef Gusteau's motto to be true to a critic named Ego.

Round Two Guess As to the Inspirational Movie:

_____

MOVIE TWENTY-EIGHT

Level Two Hints:

- The inspirational film has a male antagonist named Alfredo Linguini.
- Film critic Anton Ego orders Chateau Cheval Blanc 1947, which is an actual wine, known as an excellent vintage worth at least $2,000 USD.
- Don't eat your cheese too fast or else Remy will have to teach you about food.
- The famed Chef Thomas Keller of the breathtaking French Laundry restaurant taught the film team about the art of cooking and had a cameo role as a patron of the first restaurant.
- The Calamari motorcycle that Colette rides is styled after an actual brand which has riders known as "squids", who often sport "Team Calamari" shirts and bumper stickers.

Round Three Guess As to the Inspirational Movie:

MOVIE TWENTY-EIGHT

Level Three Hints:

- Ratatouille
- The deceased famous Chef Auguste Gusteau's first name is an anagram of his last name.
- The character of Chef Skinner was modeled Louis de Funès, a famous French comedic actor with a great range of facial expressions who was popular throughout Europe for his energetic style which included impatience and selfishness in over 130 roles in films and over 100 roles on stage during the 18 years of his career.

Round Four Guess As to the Inspirational Movie:

MOVIE TWENTY-NINE

Course #1: Frisée Salad with Lardons & Poached Eggs

Ingredients:
6 slices thick-cut bacon

1 Tbsp shallots, minced

1 Tbsp lemon juice

2 tsp Dijon mustard

2 Tbsp olive oil

4 eggs

6 cups frisée (if not available, then use romaine, spring
	varietals salad mix, or baby varietals salad mix)

1/4 tsp salt

1/8 tsp ground black pepper

Directions:
Step 1:

In a pan, on medium heat, add bacon, then cook 3 minutes.

Step 2:

Flip bacon over, then cook 3 minutes, until crispy.

Step 3:
Transfer to cutting board. Dice 1/4". Set aside.

Step 4:
Transfer 2 Tbsp bacon fat / drippings to a bowl.

Step 5:
Add shallots, lemon juice, and mustard, then whisk to mix.

Step 6:
While whisking vigorously and continuously, slowly drizzle in oil to form an emulsion. Set aside.

Step 7:
In a pot, on medium-high heat, add 3 quarts of water, then heat until boiling.

Step 8:
Reduce heat to medium, until simmering (almost boiling but not at full boil).

Step 9:
Add carefully cracked eggs by gently slipping these into the water, then cook 2 minutes, until start to get firm.

Step 10:
With slotted spoon, remove eggs carefully and set aside.

Step 11:
To bowl with dressing, add greens, then toss to coat.

Step 12:
Divide greens in equal amounts to serving plates.

Step 13:
Sprinkle to add bacon in equal amounts on salad mix.

Step 14:
Sprinkle to add salt and pepper on top of salad mix.

Step 15:
Add poached eggs, then break yolks.

Fresh / Frozen Storage:
Do NOT store.

Your Notes:

_____

MOVIE TWENTY-NINE

Course #2: Salmon in Basil Sauce served with Lemon Couscous

Basil Sauce Ingredients:
1 cup fresh basil, stemmed and chopped
1/2 cup extra virgin olive oil
1 tsp garlic, minced
2 tsp lemon juice
1/4 tsp salt

Basil Sauce Directions:
Step 1:
In a food processor or blender, add basil, olive oil, garlic, lemon juice, and salt, then blend, until pureed. Set aside.

Lemon Couscous Ingredients:
1 &1/4 cups chicken stock / broth
3/4 cup uncooked couscous
2 Tbsp butter
2 Tbsp fresh parsley, stemmed and chopped finely
2 Tbsp lemon juice
1 tsp lemon zest

1/4 tsp salt

1/8 tsp ground black pepper

Lemon Couscous Directions:

Step 1:

In a pot on medium high heat, add chicken stock, then cook, until boiling.

Step 2:

Add couscous and butter, then stir to mix well.

Step 3:

Cover with lid, then remove from heat and place on a heat-safe surface, such as a cold burner. Set aside for 5 minutes

Step 4:

Add parsley, lemon juice, zest, salt, and pepper, then stir to mix well. Re-cover with lid, then set aside.

Salmon Ingredients:
4 salmon 6 oz fillets

2 Tbsp olive oil

1/2 tsp salt

1/4 tsp ground black pepper

Salmon Directions:
Step 1:

Sprinkle to add salt and pepper to salmon fillets on both sides. Set aside.

Step 2:

In a pan, on medium heat, add oil and salmon. Cook for 4 minutes.

Step 3:

Flip fish fillets over, then cook for 4 minutes.

Check each salmon fillet by using a fork to gently pull back on a small area on the thickest part of each fillet to make sure it separates into flakes all the way through. If a fillet does not pass the test, then cook a few more minutes and recheck.

Step 4:
When done, remove salmon pan from heat, and place on a heat-safe surface, such as a cold burner. Set aside.

Assembly Directions:
Step 1:
To serving plates, add couscous, in equal amounts.

Step 2:
Add fillets, 1 to each plate. Set aside.

Step 3:
Transfer basil sauce into the hot pan that the salmon was removed from, then on medium heat, cook for 1 minute.

Step 4:
Pour warmed sauce over plated fillets, in equal amounts.

Fresh / Frozen Storage:
Do NOT store.

Your Notes:

MOVIE TWENTY-NINE

Course #3: Chocolate Pots de Crème

Pots de Crème Ingredients:
1 & 3/4 cups dairy heavy whipping cream
4 oz bittersweet chocolate, chopped
4 eggs, separated, yolks kept
1/4 cup sugar

Whipped Topping Ingredients:
1/3 cup dairy heavy whipping cream
1 Tbsp sugar
1 tsp vanilla extract

Directions:
Step 1:
Preheat oven to 325 degrees.

Step 2:
In a pot, on medium heat, add cream and bring to simmer (almost boiling but not at full boil).

Step 3:
Remove pot from heat and place on a heat-safe surface, such as a cold burner.

Step 4:
Add chocolate, then stir, until chocolate is completely melted. Set aside.

Step 5:
In a bowl, add yolks and sugar, then whisk, until light and creamy.

Step 6:
While whisking continuously, slowly drizzle to add chocolate mixture. (Adding too quickly will result in scrambled eggs!)

Step 7:
Pour through a fine mesh strainer, to add equal amounts to ramekins.

Step 8:

Transfer 4 ramekins into a baking pan with space left around each. Add water into the baking pan until comes up 2" on the outer side of the ramekins. This creates a "water bath" for the custard.

Step 9:

Cover entire pan with aluminum foil.

Step 10:

Place the baking pan with water and ramekins set into the preheated oven, on the middle rack. Bake for 35 minutes, until custard is set on edges but center still moves slightly.

Step 11:

Remove pan set from oven and place on a heat-safe surface, such as your stovetop.

Step 12:

Remove ramekins from the pan and place on a towel, to dry the outside of each.

Step 13:
Cover each ramekin with plastic wrap / film, and place in refrigerator.

Step 14:
In a mixing bowl, add cream, then using a hand or stand mixer, on high speed, beat, until doubled in volume.

Step 15:
Add sugar and vanilla extract, then beat, until holds stiff peaks.

Checking for stiff peaks:
Stiff peaks are formed when you quickly dip the mixing beaters in and out once, pulling up some of the mixture into a peak, then it stays in the peak shape and does not fall down – like the topping of a meringue pie.

Step 16:
Gently add whipped cream to top of each ramekin, taking care not to deflate the whipped cream.

Step 17:
Serve immediately.

Fresh Storage:

Cover with plastic wrap / film and store in the refrigerator. Use within 1 day.

Frozen Storage:

Do NOT freeze.

Your Notes:

_____

_____

Round One Guess As to the Inspirational Movie:

_____

MOVIE TWENTY-NINE

Level One Hint:

- The inspired dish is discussed by the female Chef protagonist as something that appears to not be a big deal to put on a menu but that takes a great deal of careful work with spices, like all of her highly flavorful recipes that are not dependent upon exotic ingredients.

Round Two Guess As to the Inspirational Movie:

_____

MOVIE TWENTY-NINE

Level Two Hints:

- The female protagonist gives cooking lessons to her therapist, and he is amazed that she can taste a dessert and know that he didn't use the specific sugar she had told him.
- The female protagonist is the Chef at Lido, a gourmet restaurant in Hamburg, Germany.
- Lina tries to run away to Italy when she is told that she cannot go to the restaurant anymore.
- This Chef's kitchen produces amazing food with precision for distinguishing palates, but spaghetti is really the way to a child's heart, as Mario and Lina prove.

Round Three Guess As to the Inspirational Movie:

_____

MOVIE TWENTY-NINE

Level Three Hints:

- Salmon in Basil Sauce served with Lemon Couscous
- Someone makes a choice about living in grey Germany over living in sunny Italy.
- Sous Mario plays eclectic jazz in the kitchen.
- While German is spoken, the message of food and family is universal, so the film has been adapted into versions in the US and in Spain.
- The Sous Chef actor could not speak German well enough for the film, so his lines are dubbed by Frank Glaubrecht, who is credited for being the German voice in 26 films and video games, dubbed for Pierce Brosnan, Mel Gibson, Al Pacino, Kevin Costner, Jeremy Irons, Christopher Walken, and Richard Gere.

Round Four Guess As to the Inspirational Movie:

_____

MOVIE THIRTY

Course #1: Deviled Bacon Eggs

Ingredients:

8 eggs

1 tsp Dijon mustard

1/3 cup mayonnaise

1/8 tsp salt

1/8 tsp ground black pepper

1 green onion, minced, finely, (both green and white
   parts)

3 slices bacon

paprika (for garnish)

Directions:

Step 1:

In a pot, add eggs and cold tap water, enough water to cover eggs plus 1".

Step 2:

Set heat to medium, then bring to a full boil.

Step 3:
Remove from heat and place on a heat-safe surface, such as a cold burner.

Step 4:
Cover pot with lid, then set aside for 12 minutes.

Step 5:
Transfer eggs to a bowl, add cold tap water and ice, until eggs are covered. Set aside for 5 minutes.

Step 6:
Tap an egg on a flat surface.

Step 7:
Roll egg on a flat surface to loosen the shell, then pick shell off, until removed completely.

Step 8:
Rinse egg under cold running water to ensure all shell bits are removed. Set aside.

Step 9:
Repeat Steps 6 – 8 for all remaining eggs.

Step 10:
Cut an egg in half, lengthwise from the skinny tip.

Step 11:
Gently remove the yolk and transfer to a bowl. Set the white aside to use later.

Step 12:
Repeat Steps 10 & 11 for all remaining eggs.

Step 13:
To yolks, add mayonnaise, mustard, salt, and pepper, then with a fork, mash thoroughly, until a consistent mixture.

Step 14:
Add onion, then stir to mix. Set aside.

Step 15:
In a pan, medium heat, add bacon, then cook for 3 minutes.

Step 16:
Flip bacon over, then cook for 3 minutes.

Step 17:
Transfer to a cutting board, then cut into small pieces or crumble apart.

Step 18:
Add bacon pieces to mixture, then stir to mix well.

Step 19:
Portion equal amounts into the "bowls" of the cut eggs.

Step 20:
Sprinkle to add paprika over eggs.

Step 21:
Place eggs on a serving plate, then cover with plastic wrap / film.

Fresh Storage:
Cover with plastic wrap / film and store in the refrigerator. Use within 2 days.

Your Notes:

_____

MOVIE THIRTY

Course #2: Korean BBQ Lettuce Cups

Slaw Ingredients:

1 oz peanut butter

1 & 1/2 tsp sesame oil

4 oz rice vinegar

1/2 tsp salt

1 Tbsp sugar

6 oz vegetable oil

2 cups cabbage mix (or Napa)

Slaw Directions:

Step 1:

In a bowl, add peanut butter, sesame oil, vinegar, salt and sugar, then whisk to mix well.

Step 2:

While whisking vigorously and continuously, slowly drizzle in oil to form an emulsion.

Step 3:

Add cabbage mix, then toss to coat evenly.

Step 4:

Cover with plastic wrap / film, then place in refrigerator, to chill.

Korean BBQ Sauce Ingredients:

5 cloves garlic, peeled

1 &1 1/2" ginger root, peeled

3 Tbsp San-G (soya) sauce

3 Tbsp chili paste

1 & 1/2 Tbsp rice vinegar

1 Tbsp sesame oil

1 Tbsp honey

Korean BBQ Sauce Directions:

Step 1:

In a blender or food processor, add garlic and ginger, then process, until ginger and garlic are very finely minced.

Step 2:

Add soy sauce, chili paste, vinegar, sesame oil, and honey, then pulse, until fully mixed.

Step 3:

Transfer to a bowl. To use soon, set aside OR To use within 1 day, cover with plastic wrap / film and place in refrigerator.

Chicken Ingredients:

1 Tbsp vegetable oil

4 chicken 6 oz boneless, skinless breasts, fresh or thawed

1/2 tsp salt

1/4 tsp ground black pepper

Chicken Directions:

Step 1:

Preheat oven to 350 degrees.

Step 2:

To a baking pan, add vegetable oil, then swirl around to coat bottom of pan.

Step 3:
Add chicken, then sprinkle to add salt and pepper.

Step 4:
Place baking pan in preheated oven, on the middle rack.
Bake for 20 minutes, until internal temperature reaches
180 degrees on your thermometer.

Step 5:
Remove baking pan from oven and place on a heat-safe
surface, such as your stovetop. Set aside 5 minutes.

Assembly:
1 head iceberg lettuce, cored and separated whole
        leaves, ensuring at least 2 leaves per person

Step 1:
Transfer chicken to a cutting board. Cut into 1/8"
slices, slicing against the grain of the meat.

Step 2:
Add to Korean BBQ Sauce bowl, then mix to coat.

Step 3:
Retrieve whole lettuce leaves and slaw from refrigerator, then place near assembly area.

Step 4:
Place an equal amount of slaw to the center of a lettuce leaf, then add equal amount of Korean BBQ chicken.

Step 5:
Transfer to a serving plate, then set aside.

Step 6:
Repeat Steps 4 & 5 for all remaining lettuce leaves.

Fresh Storage:
Cover unassembled ingredients separately with plastic wrap / film or place in a plastic sealable bag and store in the refrigerator. Use within 3 days.

Frozen Storage:
Do NOT freeze.

Your Notes:

MOVIE THIRTY

Course #3: Red Velvet Cupcakes

Red Velvet Cupcake Ingredients:

2 & 1/2 cups cake flour

2 Tbsp unsweetened cocoa

1 & 1/2 tsp salt

3/4 tsp baking powder

3/4 tsp baking soda

3/4 cup butter, softened

2 cups sugar

3 eggs

2 Tbsp **natural** red food coloring

2 tsp vanilla extract

1 & 1/2 cups dairy buttermilk

2 regular-size muffin pans (12 muffin capacity each)

24 disposable paper muffin baking cups / liners

Red Velvet Cupcake Directions:

Step 1:

Preheat oven to 350 degrees.

Step 2:
Place a muffin liner in each muffin cup. Set aside.

Step 3:
In a bowl, add flour, cocoa, salt, baking powder, and baking soda, then whisk to mix well. Set aside.

Step 4:
In a mixing bowl, add butter and sugar, then using a hand or stand mixer, medium speed, mix, until light and fluffy.

Step 5:
Add 1 egg, then mix well.

Step 6:
Repeat Step 5 for all remaining eggs.

Step 7:
Add food coloring and vanilla extract, then mix well.

Step 8:
Add 1/3 of the flour mixture, then on low speed, mix well.

Step 9:
Add 1/3 of buttermilk, then on low speed, mix well.

Step 10:
Repeat Steps 8 & 9, for all remaining flour and buttermilk.

Step 11:
Transfer batter in equal amounts to lined muffin pans.

Step 12:
Place muffin pans in the preheated oven, side by side, on the middle rack. Bake for 20 minutes.

Step 13:
Check at the center of 1 muffin in each pan, with a toothpick inserted straight down and for approximately 3/4 the length of the toothpick, then wiggle the toothpick a bit to make a hole large enough to not scrape the edges of the toothpick as it is removed. If done, then the toothpick should be "clean" or dry after removed, without wet batter sticking to it. (If not "clean", then bake a few minutes more and recheck. Repeat until "clean".)

Step 14:
Remove muffin pans from oven, then place on a wire rack to cool for 15 minutes.

Step 15:
Remove cupcakes from muffin pans and place on a flat, clean, dry work surface. Set aside.

Cream Cheese Frosting Ingredients:
16 oz cream cheese, softened
6 Tbsp butter, softened
1 &1/2 tsp vanilla extract
5 cups confectioner's (powdered) sugar

Cream Cheese Frosting Directions:
Step 1:
In a mixing bowl, add cream cheese and butter, then using hand or stand mixer, on medium speed, mix, until creamy.

Step 2:
Add vanilla extract, then on low speed, mix well.

Step 3:
Add sugar gradually, using low speed, mixing well, until all sugar is mixed in well and frosting is light and fluffy.

Step 4:
Using a frosting "knife" (rounded tip and not sharp) OR a frosting/pastry spatula, place a dollop of frosting in the middle of the top of a cupcake.

Step 5:
Using frosting knife, stay in touch with the frosting to spread it from the middle to cover the cupcake close to the edges. Do not touch the cupcake surface directly with the frosting knife. Make the frosting fairly level, adding more frosting if needed. Set aside on a serving plate.

Step 6:
Repeat Steps 4 & 5 for all remaining cupcakes.

Fresh Storage:

Cover loosely with plastic wrap / film or place a plastic or glass "dome" over the cupcakes and store in the refrigerator. You can use toothpicks inserted in just far enough in each one to keep the toothpick upright, then "tent" the plastic wrap / film overtop to keep it from touching the cupcakes and disturbing the frosting. Use within 3 days.

Frozen Storage:

Do NOT freeze.

Your Notes:

_____

_____

Round One Guess As to the Inspirational Movie:

_____

MOVIE THIRTY

Level One Hint:

- The inspired dish is served at a wedding reception in the form of an armadillo.

Round Two Guess As to the Inspirational Movie:

_____

MOVIE THIRTY

Level Two Hints:

- Shrimp Bake is served at the fair, dished up by a female principal.
- CuppaCuppa Cake is a real dessert that you make by adding a cup of one thing and a cup of something else, etc.
- There are certain things you don't say to Shelby's mother, especially when she is marinating 50lbs of crab claws.
- A local baker in Natchitoches, Louisiana (the location used to represent Chinquapin) provided the cakes for the wedding reception, making several of each for the multiple "takes" where the cakes are used during dialogue.

Round Three Guess As to the Inspirational Movie:

MOVIE THIRTY

Level Three Hints:

- The movie is based on a Broadway play that opened in 2005 and ran for 136 shows, with no on-stage male parts and was based upon the writer's sister's last 3 years of life.
- This film has six female principal parts.
- One of the female protagonists has her dream of a child fulfilled but later dies from complications from diabetes.
- The owner of the beauty parlor has strong opinions, including one about women who fix their own hair.
- When one of the female protagonists is in the child-birthing process, the father-to-be hitches a ride to the hospital on a motorcycle while wearing a bunny costume.

Round Four Guess As to the Inspirational Movie:

Index

Entrees:

291 Baked Walleye served with Caramelized Carrots

306 BBQ Beef Brisket

255 Beef Bourguignon

186 Black & Blue Mussels served with
Herbed Gnocchi

475 Brazilian Pan-Seared Steak served with
Wild Mushroom Ragoût

118 Butter Chicken served with Basmati Rice

150 Chicken Marsala

457 Chicken Salad with Goat Cheese served with
Balsamic Vinaigrette Dressing

489 Chinese-BBQ Pork

224 Fish Tacos served with Mango & Banana Salsa

173 Greek Meatballs served with
Sauce and Vermicelli

578 Korean BBQ Lettuce Cups

390 Lamb Stew with Dried Plums

81 Mayan Cocoa Chicken Mole

278 Moqueca de Camarão
aka Brazilian Shrimp Stew

375 Mushroom Ravioli

134 Peking Duck Pancakes

504 Pizza Napoletana

407 Pork Chops served with Greens in a
Cherries & Port Wine Reduction

359 Puerco Pibil

542 Ratatouille

102 Saag Paneer

562 Salmon in Basil Sauce served with
Lemon Couscous

333 Salmon served with
Lemon Crème Fraiche Sauce

348 Sausage and Peppers served with Pasta

442 Sea Scallops served with
Asparagus & Tangerine Sauce

527 Shepherd's Pie

426 Shrimp Sunset Sauté served with
Angel Hair Pasta

204 Spaghetti & Meatballs served with
Marinara Sauce & with Garlic Bread

239 Timpano

Desserts:

142 Almond Float with Cherries

229 Apricot Flan

363 Aztec Éclair Puffs

429 Beignets

338 Blackberry & Peach Cream Crumble

479 Blueberry "Caviar" served with Baked Brie

411 Bourbon Pecan Tart

311 Browned Butter Carrot Cake with
Cream Cheese Frosting

87 Caramelized Pears in Puff Pastry

547 Chocolate Cake with Chocolate Frosting

531 Chocolate Digestive Biscuit with Builder's Tea

566 Chocolate Pots de Crème

394 Cinnamon Mouse with Orange Segments

446 Crème Brûlée with Orange

154 English Trifle

296 Fry Bread

193 Gold & Amber Bread Pudding with
Pecan Sauce

259 Italian Crème Cake with
Italian Buttercream Frosting

123 Lime & Ginger Cookies

106 Melon Soup

494 New Year Cookies

281 Orange Flan

382 Panna Cotta with Fresh Berries

177 Plum & Almond Crumble

351 Plum Grappa Granita

583 Red Velvet Cupcakes

248 Strawberry Ice Cream

461 Tiramisu

510 White Russian Pie

212 Zabaglione

MIM Trivia Game Answers

Movie One: Chocolat
Movie Two: Today's Special
Movie Three: Cooking With Stella
Movie Four: Eat Drink Man Woman
Movie Five: Love's Kitchen
Movie Six: A Touch of Spice
Movie Seven: Dinner Rush
Movie Eight: Lady and The Tramp
Movie Nine: Tortilla Soup
Movie Ten: Big Night
Movie Eleven: Julie & Julia
Movie Twelve: Woman On Top
Movie Thirteen: Smoke Signals
Movie Fourteen: Planet Terror
Movie Fifteen: Soul Food
Movie Sixteen: The Godfather
Movie Seventeen: Once Upon A Time In Mexico
Movie Eighteen: Twilight
Movie Nineteen: The Hunger Games
Movie Twenty: Fried Green Tomatoes
Movie Twenty-One: Forrest Gump
Movie Twenty-Two: Last Holiday
Movie Twenty-Three: No Reservations
Movie Twenty-Four: Titanic
Movie Twenty-Five: The God of Cookery
Movie Twenty-Six: Eat Pray Love
Movie Twenty-Seven: The Best Exotic Marigold Hotel
Movie Twenty-Eight: Ratatouille
Movie Twenty-Nine: Mostly Martha
Movie Thirty: Steel Magnolias